Chris van Uffelen

Malls &
Department Stores

Chris van Uffelen

Malls &
Department Stores

BRAUN

CONTENTS

CONTENTS

Real Shopping
by Chris van Uffelen

A lot has changed since the first edition of "Malls and Department Stores" was published. Five years ago, shopping malls were located either in the suburbs or the city center, but both types housed shops and department stores; the two main protagonists in the battle for customer favor. Nowadays, online shopping claims a large percentage of the market and is of far greater significance than a printed mail order catalogue ever was. Over the past few years a new trend has emerged, where online traders open stores on the high street or in shopping malls that serve simply as showrooms and consultation areas. Traditional shops have also started to offer free delivery in order to keep up with the online competition.

However, neither small independent shops nor gigantic online shops are the subject of this book. This volume concentrates on a huge range of different kinds of stores and products and the environment in which they are sold, as well as the design of these

places as 'shopping experiences'. Many architectural styles can be identified, everything from a simple neighborhood mall near a city park to a mega-mall in an undeveloped area between cities. These businesses share some similarities in that they are all much larger than an independent store and offer a wide range of different products. The owner of a small store arranges "their" store in a way that best targets the intended audience. In the case of a shopping mall, however, the owner or operator of the building is rarely also the operator of an individual store. The property manager furnishes the building in such a way as to please the majority of his future tenants, who in turn hope to gain some of the shoppers attracted by the center as a whole. The anticipation and definition of design efficiency in this scenario is, for this reason, more abstract than in an independent store. In the past, a department store could be defined as a spatially continuous entity, in contrast to a shopping center, which comprised enclosed units housing independent businesses. Nowadays, this definition has become obsolete thanks to new concepts, such as the shop-within-a-shop design often implemented by department stores.

Likewise, the difference between a market (groceries or specialized products) and a general store (wide range of goods) has also all but disappeared. Public access is yet another criteria that can no longer be used for the purpose of definition. Over the last few decades, shopping centers have been established in the fashion industry in France that are only open to retailers.

At the beginning everything was so clear. Originally, sales space was organized according to product. For example a bakery with its own café is an example of this that remains today. However, the separation of production and sales can be traced back to the antiquity, for example with the Greek agora and the closed Roman basilica. In the Middle Ages, stores were often located on the ground floor of town halls or townhouses. These shops were often specialty stores selling typical regional products, such as the Cloth Hall in Ypres. The basilica building form gained in importance once again during the 19th century, particularly in the case of market hall architecture. Baltard's former hall in Paris is one of the best-known examples of this. Such halls, housing different suppliers all

↖ | **Hermann Blankenstein: Market hall I at Alexanderplatz, Berlin,** 1886, functional market hall in the center of Berlin
↖ | **Henri Sauvage: Le grand magasin La Samaritaine, Paris,** 1933, Art Déco architecture along the Seine waterfront still with large windows

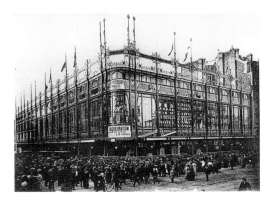

under one roof, can be seen as the predecessor to the shopping center, even though the products on offer were not universal, but rather focused on groceries. Other products were usually sold in the passages rather than the market halls. These areas were also roofed and accommodated shops selling a wide range of goods. The construction of department stores also began in the 19th century, selling a range of products from different manufacturers. Paris was a pioneer in this new development: gaudy but lavishly glazed palace façades and domes that drew light deep into the building characterized the building form of the Grand Magasins. These three building types served large-scale shopping until the mid-20th century, albeit with stylistic variations and changing furnishings.

The appearance of commercial buildings changed dramatically during the post-WWII period. The increasingly stylized use of electrical light became an important characteristic of department stores and large-scale glazing soon gave way to a closed façade, with the exception of a large display window. At the same time, the shopping mall made its appearance in the USA, replacing the so-called 'power centers', similar in design to the English retail parks, with an introverted, weather-proof complex. Victor Gruen's Southdale in Edina near Minneapolis is considered to be the first examples of mall architecture: linear, covered and introverted. This was

built to serve the rapidly growing urban sprawl, which grew as a result of tax advantages that came with real estate depreciation and the high numbers of car owners. Shopping centers took on the role of artificial city centers, playing a part in providing space for leisure activities with the necessary gastronomic amenities. For many years these large shopping malls developed both as a result of these economical factors and as a response to competition from inner-city malls. Shopping centers of various sizes were able to develop independently of any historical context: From a neighborhood center with a 3–5 kilometer catchment area housing a population of around 40,000, to regional, super-regional, and all the way to a so-called mega-mall that serves an area with a radius of 165 kilometers and houses more than six departments stores as its anchor stores.

The term mega-mall was first applied to the Canadian West Edmonton Mall, which also inspired the category of mega-multi malls. The mall was completed in four phases (1981–1998, approx. 500,000 m^2) and has seven department stores, 800 stores, 19 movie theaters, 13 night clubs, 110 restaurants, a chapel, and a hotel as well as theme parks that create a smooth transition to the adventure park. In the mean time, the Dubai Mall (2008) has been built and is twice as big, and the Mall of Arabia will be four times as big. Anchor stores are of particular importance in these huge

shopping complexes, as these are what lure visitors to the center. If these anchor stores relocate elsewhere, the mall can enter a downward spiral, drawing fewer and fewer visitors and losing tenants, ending up as a so-called "dead mall". This phenomenon is more prevalent in suburbia than the inner city. A new modern trend involves opening the mall up to the outside, while the large glazed roofs are reminiscent of postwar architecture. Numerous malls and department stores, as well as market halls and neighborhood malls, are undergoing renovation or remodeling work in order to offer customers a new and modern shopping experience, one which online shops – not to mention mobile apps – can't hope to compete with. The local shopping trip has also become an important leisure activity and these malls show a wide range of differing architectural styles; these are presented amongst the around 100 examples in this volume.

HPP International
Planungsgesellschaft

↑ | **View of the parking deck**
→ | **Interior design**

Loop 5 Shopping Center

Weiterstadt

Loop 5, located on the A5 highway in Weiterstadt, is Germany's first themed shopping mall. The design was based on the theme of 'air travel', inspired by the close proximity of Frankfurt airport and the European Space Agency Center in Darmstadt. The complex comprises two full stories, a basement level and a staggered third story. The parking lot has nine levels, accommodating 3,000 parking spaces. The fully air conditioned mall is built as a ring mall and offers space for 150 retail locations, ranging in size from 25 to 3,420 square meters; 1,430 square meters of restaurants; and 1,200 square meters of leisure space.

PROJECT FACTS

Address: Gutenbergstraße 5, 64331 Weiterstadt, Germany. **Client:** Loop 5 Shopping Center GmbH.
Completion: 2009. **Gross floor area:** 182,940 m². **Estimated visitors:** 20,000 per day.

↑ | **Bright interior**
← | **Airplane seats**

← | Parking lot
↓ | Ground floor plan

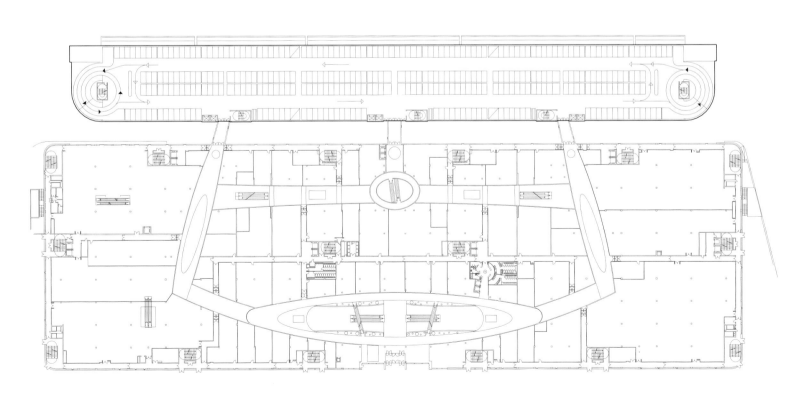

↑ | **Interior**
↘ | **Exterior,** by day and at night

↗ | **Special feature,** pool at Bernaqua Spa
→ | **The complex**

Westside Shopping and Leisure Centre

Berne

In addition to the 55 shops, 10 restaurants and bars, hotel, multiplex cinema, indoor water park with wellness center and housing, Westside radically reinvents the concept of shopping, entertainment and living. With its impressive location above Berne's A1 highway and its direct connection to the train and transport network, Westside is a meeting place for the whole greater region of Berne. The building design integrates the landscape and the different directions of the site while providing a unique look to the external areas. The concept of Westside was to create a public space offering endless amenities and services and a unique integration of architecture and landscape on a large urban scale.

Address: Riedbachstrasse 100, 3027 Berne, Switzerland. **Planning partners:** Burckhardt + Partner AG.
Structural engineers: Westside B+S Ingenieur AG, Moor Hauser & Partner AG. **Landscape architects:**
4d AG Landschaftsarchiteken. **Lighting designers:** Hefti Hess Martignoni Elektro AG. **Façade designers:** Emmer Pfenninger Partner AG. **Client:** Neue Brunnen AG. **Completion:** 2008. **Gross floor area:**
141,500 m². **Additional functions:** hotel, indoor water park, multiplex cinema, residential, wellness center.

↑ | **Roof construction,** from inside
← | **Wellness center,** swimming pool

← | Solar panels on roof
↓ | Sections

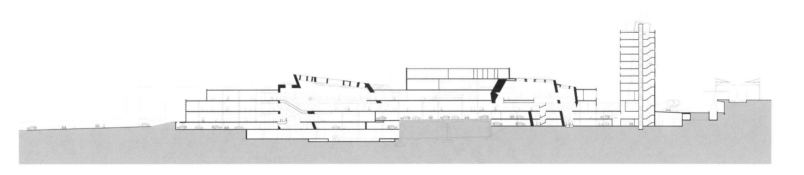

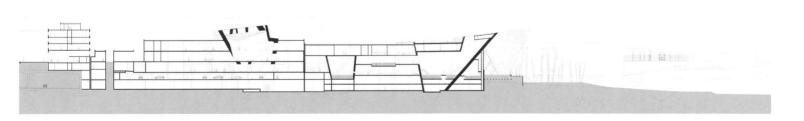

↑ | **Entrance**
↗ | **Interior view**
→ | **Shop windows,** interrupt the façade

Leiner Furniture Store and M-Preis

Innsbruck

The new Leiner furniture store can be seen from a considerable distance, approaching Innsbruck from the east. The four-story structure is a beacon, welcoming passersby. Along with the large areas of green, the angular form of the building itself makes a strong impression. Like a folded tablecloth, the translucent metal construction envelopes the volumes of the building. With this striking façade, Zechner & Zechner are taking a stand against the standardization and anonymity of current furniture store architecture. The building comprises four above-ground floors and two below-ground floors. A spiral ramp inside the building connects the display floors, allowing customers to get an overview of the store's range by just strolling through the building.

PROJECT FACTS

Address: Grabenweg 60, 6020 Innsbruck, Austria. **Client:** Kika Möbelhandels, Rudolf Leiner.
Completion: 2012. **Gross floor area:** 17,100 m².

↑ | Bright interior
← | Metal mesh façade

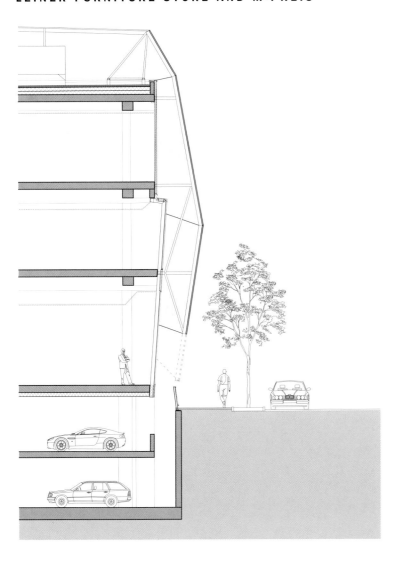

← | Section
↓ | Ground floor plan

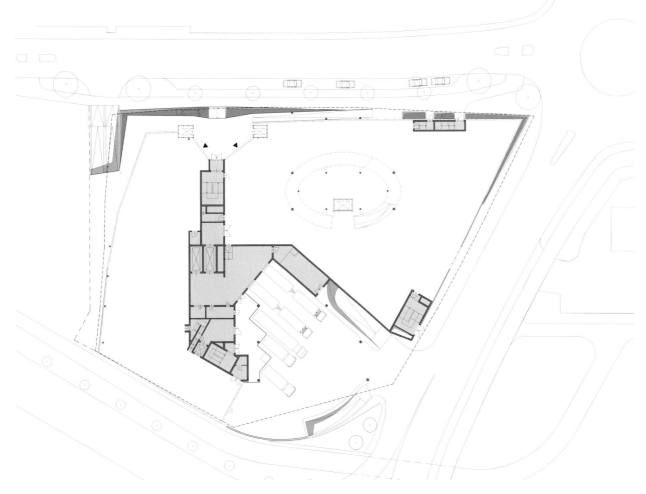

form A architekten

↑ | **Two-story volume**
↓ | **Parking area**
↘ | **Escalator**

→ | **Transparent roof,** foil cushions
↓ | **Lift,** in glass rotunda

Shopping Cité

Baden-Baden

The two-story volume of the Shopping Cité is adapted to suit the surrounding landscape, but nevertheless has a characteristic appearance thanks to its rounded form. The upper surface of the shallow dome comprises shimmering façade panels. The parking areas are located above the retail level and beneath the dome and all areas are connected by a number of escalators and lifts in glass rotundas. The rotundas are covered with a transparent roof of foil cushions, which feature integrated sun and glare protection. Curving roof sails and large skylights cover the rest of the mall.

PROJECT FACTS

Address: Gewerbepark Cité 7, 76532 Baden-Baden, Germany. **Client:** Oos-Center Baden-Baden GmbH.
Completion: 2006. **Gross floor area:** 63,800 m².

↑ | Glass, steel and concrete
← | Site plan

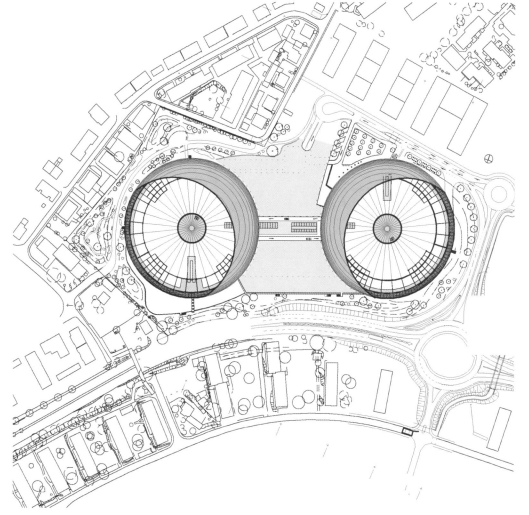

← | Adapted to suit the surrounding landscape
↓ | Ground floor plan

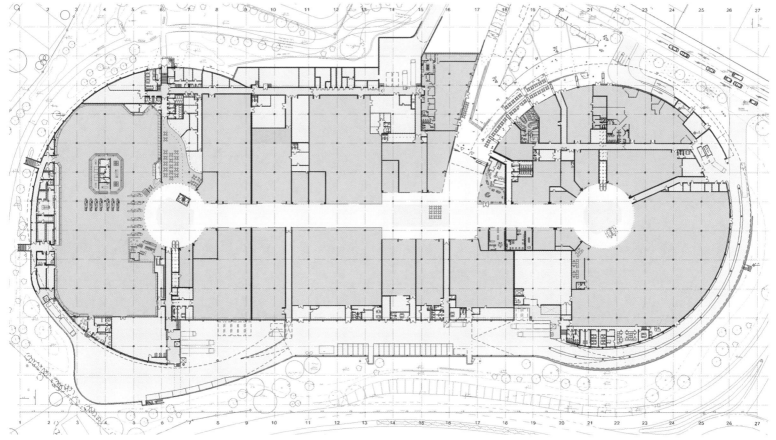

Helin & Co Architects

↑ | **Pool,** in front of buildings
→ | **Façade**

Skanssi Areal Center

Turku

The Skanssi Areal Center project design started as a winning entry in an architectural competition arranged by the city of Turku in 2003. The design concept comprises an area of six blocks, which includes residential buildings, a shopping center, two parking lots and surrounding areas. The architectural style of the Skanssi Areal Center is, above all, aesthetically interesting and very varied in terms of scale. The façades are divided into smaller parts and the use of vivid materials, such as handmade bricks and plaster give the building its dynamic appearance. In the shopping area, the plazas divide the space creating an interesting series of varied inner courts full of light. The glass roofs draw light inside and their triangular steel construction casts shadows on the walls.

PROJECT FACTS
Address: Skanssinkatu 10, 20730 Turku, Finland. **Client:** Hartela Oy. **Completion:** 2009. **Gross floor area:** 130,000 m². **Estimated visitors:** 8,770 per day. **Additional functions:** residential.

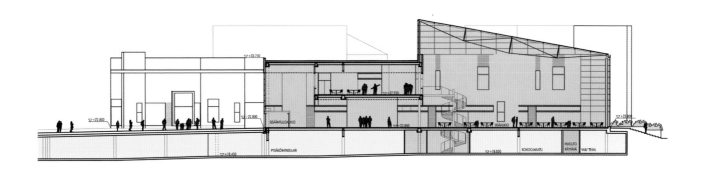

← | **Glass roof,** draws light inside
↑ | **Section**
↙ | **Ground floor plan**
↓ | **First floor plan**

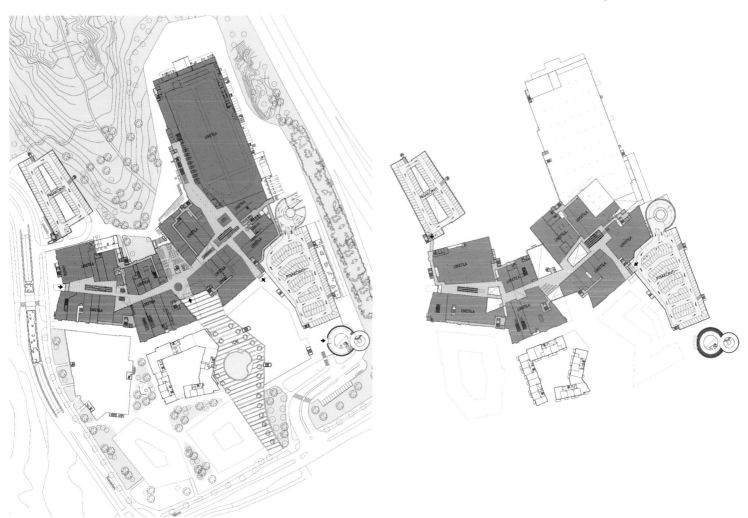

↑ | **Bird's-eye view**
↓ | **Modern interior**
↘ | **Internal gallery**
↘↘ | **Atrium,** with gallery

Jesolo Magica – Retail Center

Jesolo

The new Jesolo Magica shopping mall is located halfway between the town center and the Jesolo waterfront. The area borders the Via Roma Destra, a strategic position that makes the project a major gateway to the town. Like the petals of a flower, the volumes open up around a central space; here, the main axes of circulation traverse a gallery that has been transformed into a sheltered piazza. The new complex is sensitively scaled in harmony with its prestigious setting. Natural light and the surrounding landscape gently interact with the petal structures that make up the complex. The new Jesolo Magica center will allow the lido system to open inwards and include not only the new center, but also the neighboring areas, thus closing the areas of public and social interest of Jesolo Mare into a broader three-sided aspect.

Address: Jesolo, Italy. **Structural engineers:** Favero & Milan. **Client:** Home Group. **Completion:** ongoing. **Gross floor area:** 38,000 m². **Additional functions:** roof top restaurant.

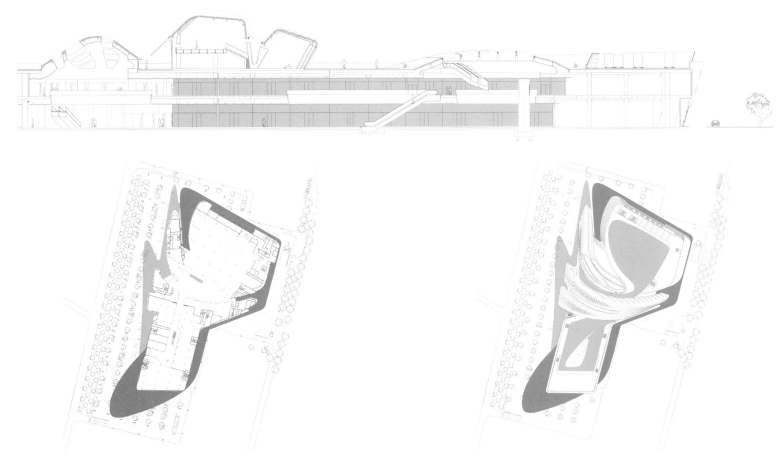

↑ | **Longitudinal section, ground floor and roof plans**
↓ | **Main entrance**

↑ | **Interior view,** entrance
↗ | **Play elements**
→ | **Family dining area,** with adult and children's tables

Westfield Family

Roseville

Designers at the award-winning, inter-disciplinary design firm Rios Clementi Hale Studios partnered with Westfield marketing professionals on design elements of the WFamily program, which is being implemented in select Westfield centers across North America. The experience is made cohesive by decorative motifs and information about natural eco-systems, such as rainforest, ocean, and mountain. The interdependence of life is a focus of the play space, which features a leaf slide, flower seat, and frog stools. Large-scale butterfly mobiles crafted from water-jet-cut aluminum hang in the atrium to signal the play space location. Design elements are also chosen to relate to the educational program. The flower seat is an extra-bright color because flowers use their brightness to survive on the rainforest floor. Among the play elements are a giant brain coral and a tube worm tunnel.

PROJECT FACTS
Address: 1151 Galleria Boulevard, Roseville, CA 95678, USA. **Original building:** Stantec Architecture.
Client: Westfield . **Completion:** 2008.

↑ | **Family lounge**
← | **Play element**

← | Shopping gallery
↙ | Elevations

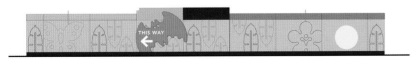

↑ | **Open space concept**
↘ | **View from parking**

↗ | **Food court,** maximizes panorama
→ | **View,** Serra de Mantiqueira

Serramar Parque Shopping

São Paulo

The proposal was to develop a mall for tourists and also for the residents in the Northern Coast of São Paulo State. The architects created an open space concept that responds to the natural surroundings. The blocks of shops are arranged in an irregular and angled shape, set apart from each other in order to allow natural ventilation. The food court has been opened out to maximizes panoramic views of the Serra da Mantiqueira. The Serramar Parque Shopping has approximately 20,000 square meters of shopping and restaurant space, housing 100 stores, including anchors shops and retail stores, as well as a supermarket, a home center, food court with fast food and family restaurants, four cinemas and 1,000 parking spaces.

PROJECT FACTS

Address: Avenida José Herculano, 1086, Caraguatatuba, São Paulo 11666-000, Brazil. **Client:** Serveng Civilsan. **Completion:** 2011. **Gross floor area:** 30,300 m². **Additional functions:** cinemas.

↑ | **Entrance**
← | **Shopping area**

← | Food court
↓ | Ground floor plan

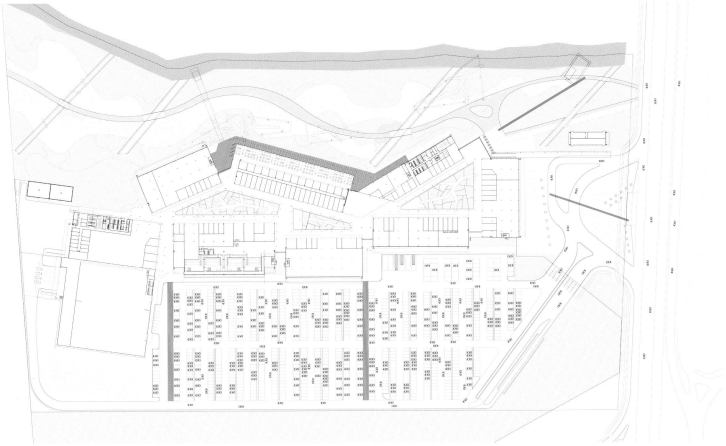

↑ | **Front view**
→ | **Elements,** arranged around a green oasis

Mondeal Retail Park

Ahmedabad

Blocher Blocher India, the Asian branch of the architecture and design office Blocher Blocher Partners, has created an ensemble that accommodates the growing demands of the Indian population. The outdoor mall is located in one of the most exclusive areas of Ahmedabad and unifies retail, service offerings and gastronomy with exceptional architecture. The design features a green and shaded plaza as well as a wide range of parking lots. The four volumes with their warm beige façades have a relatively lightweight appearance despite their monolithic cubature. This impression is also emphasized by the elongated window elements.

PROJECT FACTS   **Address:** S.G. Highway, Ahmedabad 380015, India. **Client:** HN Safal Group. **Completion:** 2012. **Gross floor area:** 25,000 m². **Estimated visitors:** 3,200 per day. **Additional functions:** offices, services.

↑ | **Green and shaded plaza**
↙ | **Ground floor plan**

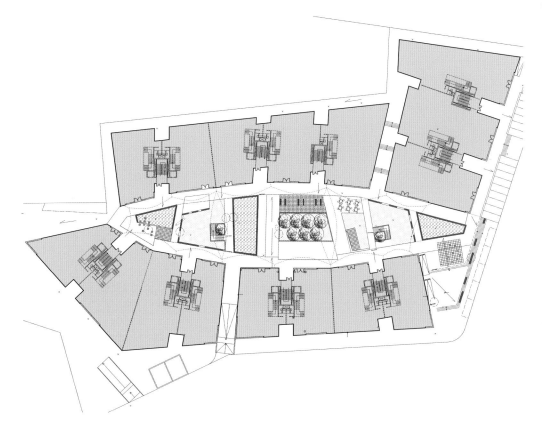

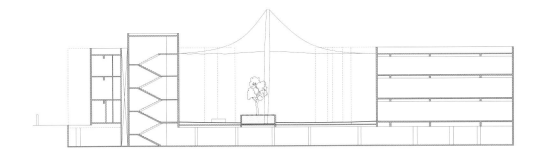

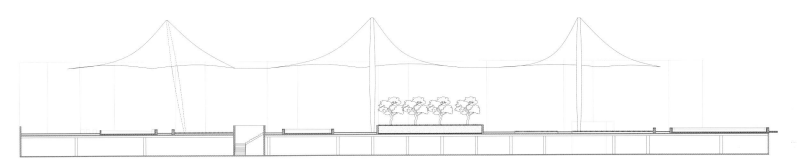

↑ | **Sections**
← | **Rhythmic façade,** comprising glass and
concrete

↑ | **Main view**
↘ | **Section**

↗ | **Street view**
↘ | **Interior**

Pedregal Shopping Center

Mexico City

This project creates a new architectural statement in the Pedregal area of Mexico City. The surrounding area is characterized by large houses and high walls, giving it a rather closed and unwelcoming appearance. The building responds to this environment with a perforated zinc façade that covers a layer of laminated glass. This opens up the building, allowing views of the interior from outside. The building comprises two commercial levels, a roof garden and two underground parking levels. This is a sustainable and intelligent development project with an automation and control system that utilizes passive and active energy saving resources.

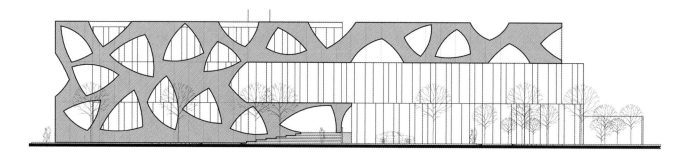

↑ | **Communal area**
← | **Interior,** with escalator

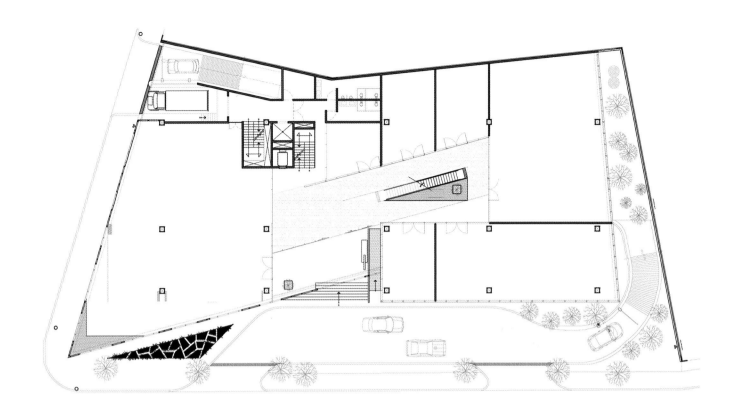

↑ | Ground floor plan
↓ | Sketch

Elliott + Associates
Architects

↑ | **Main entrance,** west elevation
→ | **Staircase**

Balliets

Oklahoma City

Balliets embodies a classically modern personality. Shaped by beautiful proportions, timeless forms and dramatic lighting, the space displays a range of elegant textures and materials. The second floor cosmetics studio is filled with natural light. The first floor houses apparel, accessories, jewelry and shoes. The seven spectacular windows feature double-sided projection screens, enabling product and event images to be projected to both the store's interior and exterior. The second floor is home to cosmetics, fragrance and sales support areas. The focus is on creating store personality.

PROJECT FACTS

Address: 5801 Northwest Grand Boulevard, Oklahoma City, OK 73118, USA. **Client:** Bob and DeDe Benham. **Completion:** 2010. **Gross floor area:** 1,570 m². **Estimated visitors:** 50 per day. **Additional functions:** seven 12 m x 12 m windows feature double-sided projection screens for advertising.

↑ | Sales area
↓ | Ground floor plan

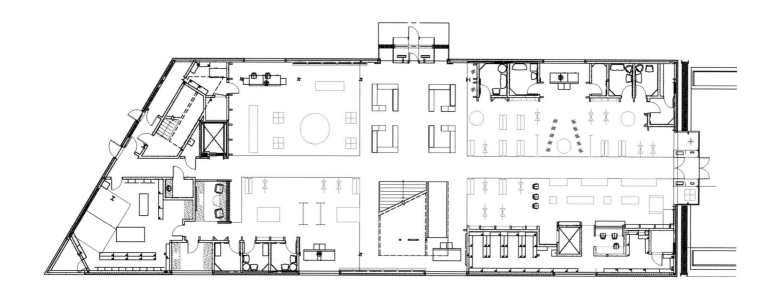

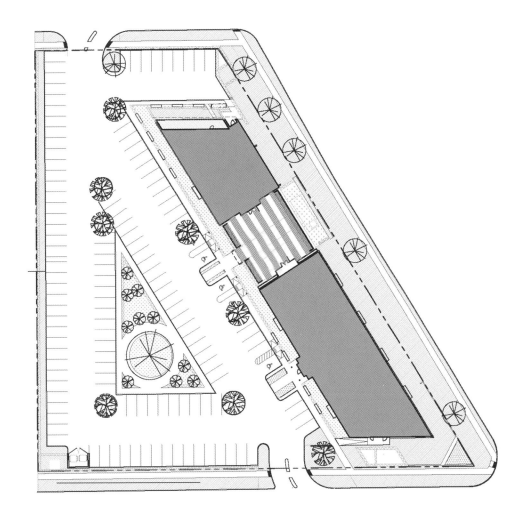

↖ | **Site plan**
↙ | **Cosmetic studio,** products
↓ | **Changing room**

GAD - Global Architectural
Development
Dara Kirmizitoprak
Architecture

↑ | **Interior view**
↗ | **Exterior view**
→ | **Bird's-eye view**

Autopia

Istanbul

Autopia is a proposal for one of the world's largest auto-malls, currently under construction in Istanbul, Turkey. The project includes 216,000 square meters of retail and service space for auto sales, spread across five floors. Every level is accessible by car, facilitating the flow of circulation within the mall. A test drive track on the roof provides a necessary amenity, given the scale of the project. Autopia is a solution to the increasing demand for retail development outside of the dense urban center. It will be the first of its kind in Turkey, introducing a new building typology to the city.

PROJECT FACTS

Address: Kirac Namik Kemal Mah, Adnan Khveci Boulevard N:1, 34357 Istanbul, Turkey. **Client:** Kelesoglu & Gul Construction. **Completion:** 2011. **Gross floor area:** 216,000 m².

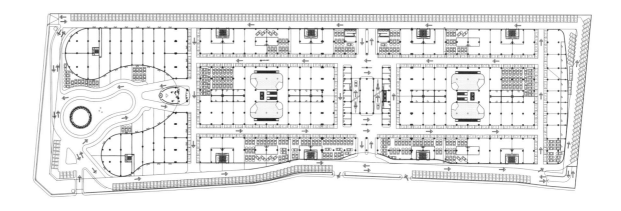

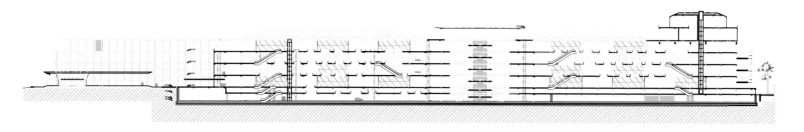

↑↑ | Ground floor plan
↑ | Section
← | Showroom

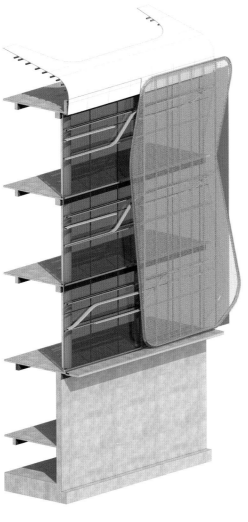

← | **Façade,** model
↓ | **View from the rear**

↑ | **Front view**
→ | **Interior view**

Daiber Convenience Store DA08

Wangen

During the planning phase of this supermarket in Wangen, a concept was developed that uses as little energy as possible both during the construction and when the supermarket is in operation. To allow daylight to be drawn into the building through the skylights, the building volume is arranged into higher and lower areas. In terms of the design, the skylights develop from the horizontally structured volume. A horizontal U highlights the entrance. A high skylight also emphasizes the entrance situation. The supermarket also incorporates a café, bakery, grocery section and cash desks. Unusual additional features, such as a drive-in bakery and café terrace with views of the Swabian Alps give this supermarket ist unique character.

Address: Siemensstraße 10, 73117 Wangen, Germany. **Completion:** 2011. **Gross floor area:** 2,500 m². **Estimated visitors:** 1,000 per day.

↑ | Context
← | Shopping aisle

← | Bakery
↓ | Ground floor plan

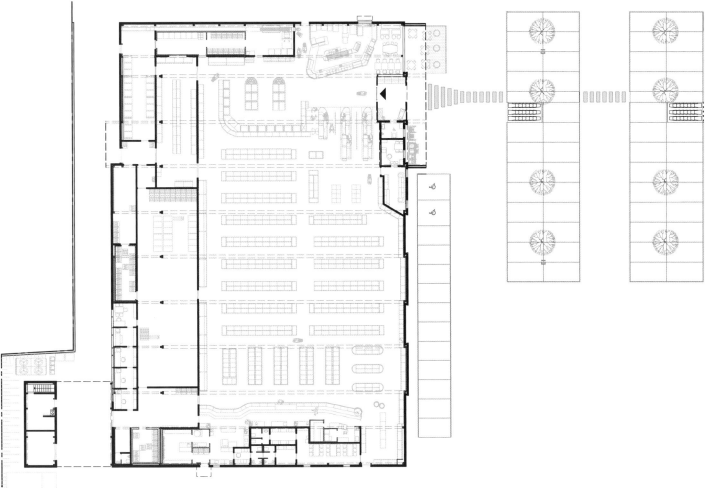

↑ | **South elevation**
↗ | **Façade,** follows lines of escalators inside
→ | **Entrance area,** at night

Shopping Center Rödertalpark

Großröhrsdorf

The Rödertalpark was built in 1993 and is one of the most commercially successful shopping centers in Dresden. The architecture and leasing situation of the building ensure a high number of customers and make the shopping center a special attraction in the region. During the planning phase, a great importance was placed on customer service and functionality. The two-story building has access to the street from every level and each entrance is highlighted by large red portals. The rest of the building exterior is relatively plain in contrast, giving the entire volume a modern appearance. The exterior is characterized by a gray and silver aluminum façade which is interrupted by glass windows and sandwich panels. Inside, the existing ground floor mall has been newly designed and a second mall has been added on the upper level.

PROJECT FACTS

Address: Pulsnitzer Straße 16, 01900 Großröhrsdorf, Germany. **Original building:** Dr. Arnold + Mener Architekturbüro, 1993. **Client:** confidential. **Completion:** 2013. **Gross floor area:** 17,898 m². **Estimated visitors:** 16,500 per day.

↑ | Sketch
↓ | Main view

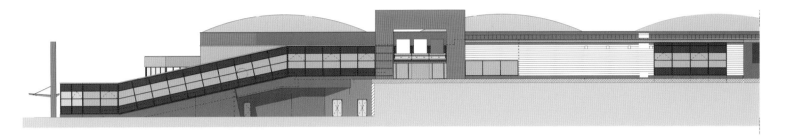

↑ | East elevation
↙ | Entrance area
↓ | Escalators

↑ | **Exterior,** transparent and opaque façade sections
↗ | **Exterior,** at night
→ | **Escalators**

Betty Blue Retail Park

Roermond

The challenge faced by these architects was to created an exclusive building on a relatively small budget. The solution was the use of a modular system. Such systems usually result in a predictable shape but in this case, the architects have used a wide variety of façade openings to give the building a more individual character. The random patterns result in a striking and dynamic design that emphasizes the modernity of the area and the shops within.

PROJECT FACTS

Address: Schaarbroekerweg 58, 6042 EJ Roermond, The Netherlands. **Client:** Van Pol Participaties, TCN Property Projects. **Completion:** 2008. **Gross floor area:** 37,000 m². **Estimated visitors:** 5,500 per day.

↑ | Aerial view
↙ | Ground floor plan

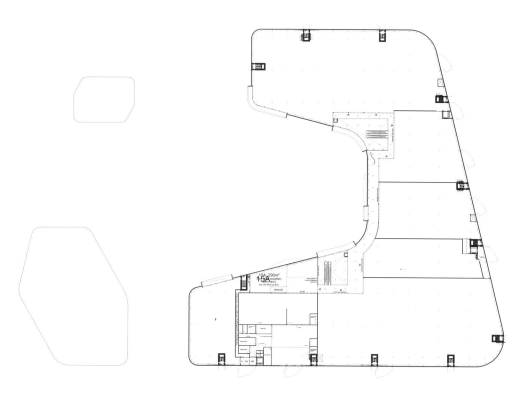

← | Escalators from above
↓ | Parking lot

Architekten Domenig &
Wallner

↑ | **Bird's-eye view**, rendering
↓ | **Parking lot**

SC Supernova

Buzin

This plot is located in Buzin, few minutes south of Zagreb, and can be divided into distinct sections: mall, towers and the "finger", which houses the office and administration area. The mall space with the parking deck appears as a calm, two-story volume. The access road is a continuation of the entrance drive and continues to the parking lot, giving the building complex a protective coherence. Self-contained glass volumes rise from the center of the mall complex. The towers serve as a landmark and orientation point for the entire area. Gently undulating and overhanging façades give the design the necessary dynamic and character. The project leader was DI Roland Heindl, who works for Architekten Domenig & Wallner.

PROJECT FACTS

Address: Buzinski Krci 1, 10010 Buzin, Croatia. **Client:** m2 Baumanagement GmbH. **Completion:** ongoing. **Gross floor area:** 145,150 m². **Additional functions:** entertainment, offices.

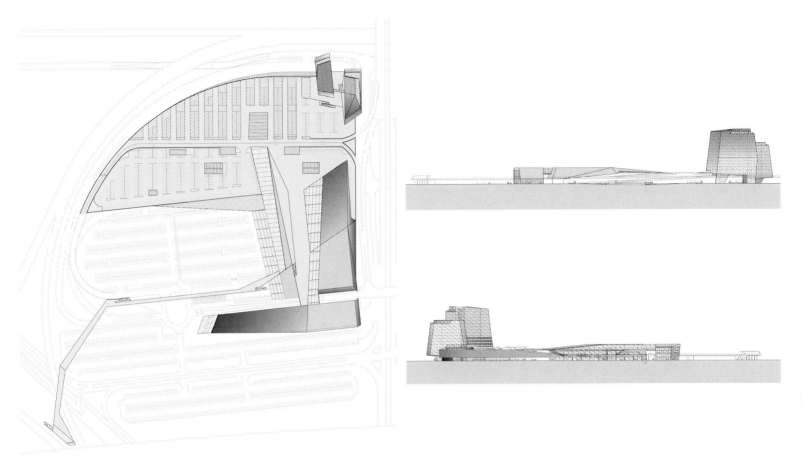

↑ | **Site plan**
↓ | **Model**

↑ | **West and east elevations**

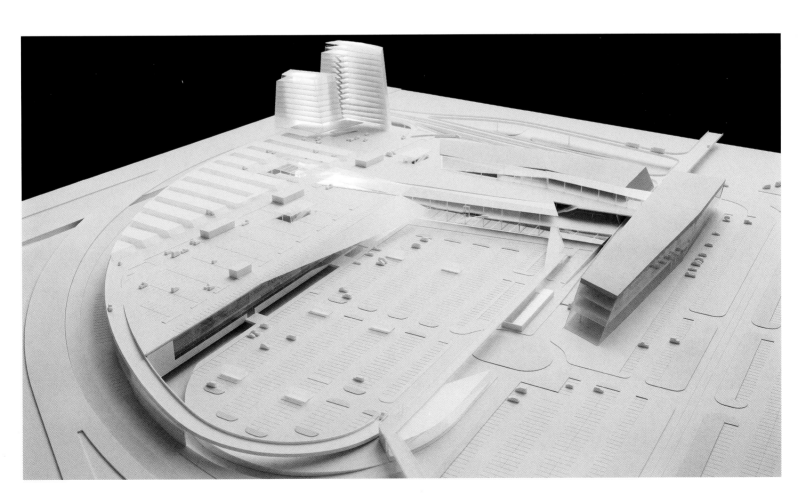

ATP Architects and
Engineers

↑ | **Entrance**
↗ | **Interior**
→ | **Parking area,** with wave-shaped timber roof
of the mall in the background

G3 Shopping Resort

Gerasdorf

A huge wave-shaped timber roof floats above the 20-meter-high and 500-meter-long mall,
part of a multifunctional timber roofscape. The design process focused on creating a ho-
mogenous and at the same time dramatic building. Despite its size the primarily single
story building nestles gently in the hilly terrain north of Vienna. This design principle is
continued in the interior: The entire spatial sequence is flooded with natural light. The
variations of form, color and material reflect the collage of the Lower Austrian landscape.
G3 was subject to an environmental impact assessment. The design paid maximum atten-
tion to economic, ecological and socio-cultural sustainability.

PROJECT FACTS

Address: G3 Platz 1, 2201 Gerasdorf, Vienna, Austria. **Landscape architects:** Kieran Fraser. **Client:** HY Immobilien Ypsilon GmbH. **Completion:** 2012. **Gross floor area:** 93,000 m².

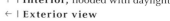

↑ | **Interior,** flooded with daylight
← | **Exterior view**

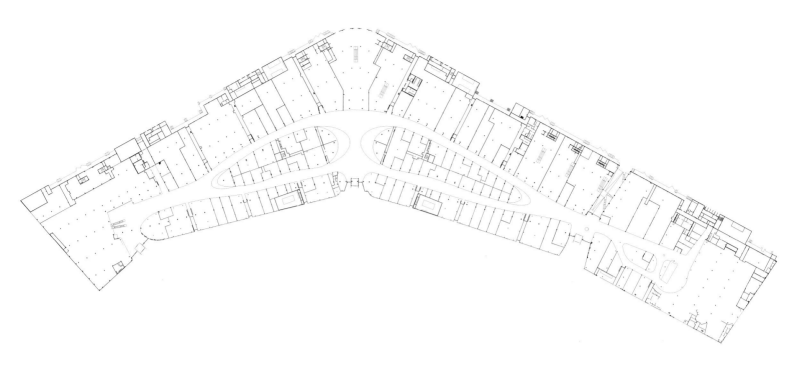

↑ | Ground floor plan
↓ | Timber roof construction

Migdal Arquitectos/Jaime Varon, Abraham Metta, Alex Metta

↑ | **Exterior façade,** covered with contemporary metal paneling
↗ | **Structural system,** based on reinforced concrete piles
→ | **Interior design,** adopts elements from the outside

Town Center

Zumpango

This shopping mall is located in a densely populated area that was poorly served in terms of the needs of the community, with no existing quality businesses. This shopping mall provides local residents with much-needed services and retail opportunities and welcomes approximately 7,000 visitors each day. Pedestrian paths have been created to connect the mall to nearby neighborhoods. Large triangular glass covers highlight the entrances and the exterior façades are covered with metal paneling, which gives the entire design a contemporary feel. The food court is an open space with a roof for protection against the weather. This has been equipped with plants and furniture in order to generate a peaceful and friendly environment.

PROJECT FACTS

Address: Carretera Los Reyes Acozac 2000, 55600 Zumpango, Mexico. **Client:** Municipality of Zumpango.
Completion: 2010. **Gross floor area:** 53,000 m². **Estimated visitors:** 7,000 per day. **Additional functions:** cinemas, gymnasium, price club.

↑ | Open-air courtyard
← | Bright, reflective interior design

↖ | Exterior view
↓ | Site plan

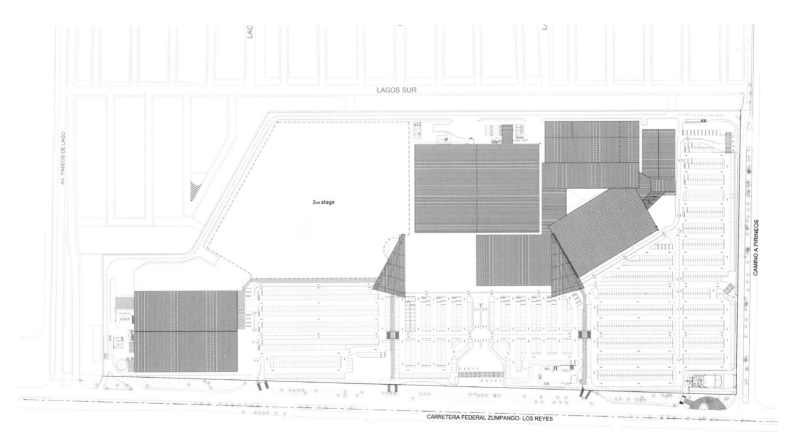

↑ | **Building,** illuminated at night
→ | **Inside,** variations of opacity diffuse the light

K:fem

Stockholm

This department store houses fashion retailers only. The building is characterized by a dramatic back-lit ceiling with white logotypes on red. The façades are similarly executed, with printed glass shifting from transparent to white in front of a red backdrop. A large hole dominates the open interior, a reverence to the circular motif that became a Vällingby icon in 1954. A smaller triangular unit in black enameled glass, dedicated to one single shop, completes the structure. A narrow passage with glazed bridges connects the two buildings to each other and with the existing grid.

PROJECT FACTS
Address: Vällingby City, Stockholm, Sweden. **Planning partners:** Centrumutveckling Håkan Karlsson AB.
Client: AB Svenska Bostäder. **Completion:** 2008. **Gross floor area:** 16,600 m².

↑ | **White flight of stairs,** brings visitors up toward the light
↙ | **Sections**

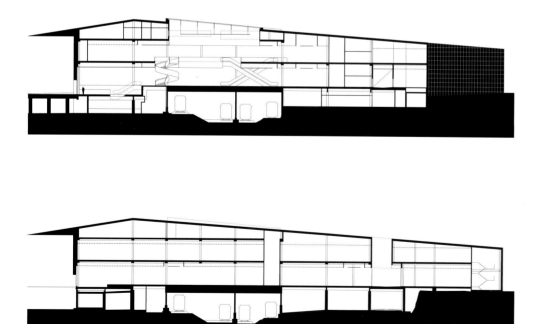

← | **Digitally controlled lighting**
↓ | **The new eye-catcher,** in Vällingby

↑ | **Exterior façade,** at night
↘ | **Main view**
↘↘ | **Interior**

↗ | **Interior,** different retail levels
→ | **Glazed roof,** draws light deep into the center

Q19

Vienna

The Samum paper factory is an historical, listed building at the end of Karl Marx Hof in Vienna. The former factory has now been renovated and combined with a new extension to create an attractive shopping center that establishes a connection between the old and the new and establishes a new quarter – Q19. Advertisements, façade and forecourt melt together to form an urban public space. Customers are welcomed into an exciting varied space, where the play between daylight and artificial light create a dynamic inner-city atmosphere.

PROJECT FACTS

Address: Grinzinger Straße 112, 1190 Vienna, Austria. **Original building:** Philipp Jakob Manz, 1909. **Client:** DHP Immobilien Leasing GmbH. **Completion:** 2005. **Gross floor area:** 54,000 m². **Estimated visitors:** 10,000 per day. **Additional functions:** billiard, car sharing, car wash, fitness studio, offices.

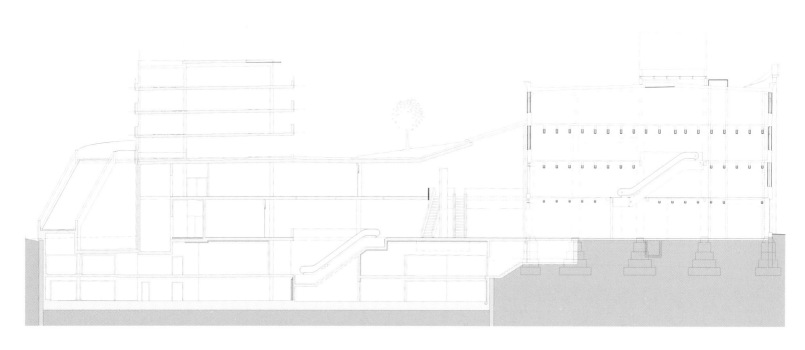

↑ | Section
↙ | Storage space
↓ | Façade detail

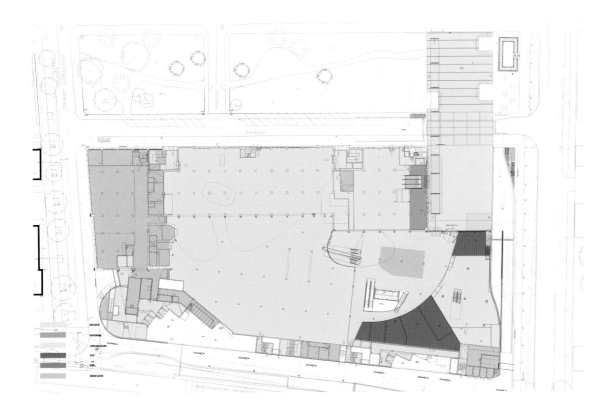

↑ | **Ground floor plan**
↓ | **Roof,** parking garage

José Fernando Gonçalves

↑ | **Main façade**
↗ | **Connection,** between parking and super-
market
→ | **Exterior view**

Supermarket

Vila Nova de Gaia

The diversity of the site's surroundings forced the proposal to shape both form and function in a way that would help face this urban challenge. The solution is restricted to a regular volume for the supermarket, with parking space underneath, an adjacent enclosed volume for storage and a third volume that connects the first two. The proposal's framework
foresaw a low-cost construction with an elementary hierarchy of materials that defines
the spatial nature of each function: reinforced concrete with metal frame and glass for the
main volume; corrugated metal for the warehouse; concrete for the ramp/elevator volume.
This elementary approach to materials and design creates a space that reacts to the predi-
catble superposition of diverse advertising elements in a way that balances the need for
a neutral support whilst, at the same time, still carrying a strong architectural identity.

PROJECT FACTS **Address:** Rua Raimundo de Carvalho, 4430-185 Vila Nova de Gaia, Portugal. **Client:** DIA Portugal Super-mercados. **Completion:** 2008. **Gross floor area:** 1,300 m².

↑ | **Main volume,** comprising concrete, metal and glass
↙ | **Site plan**

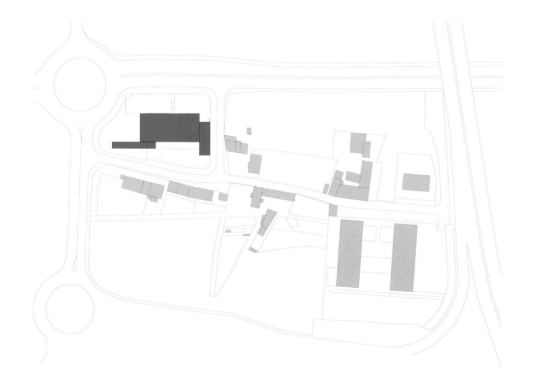

← | Interior view
↓ | Ground floor plan

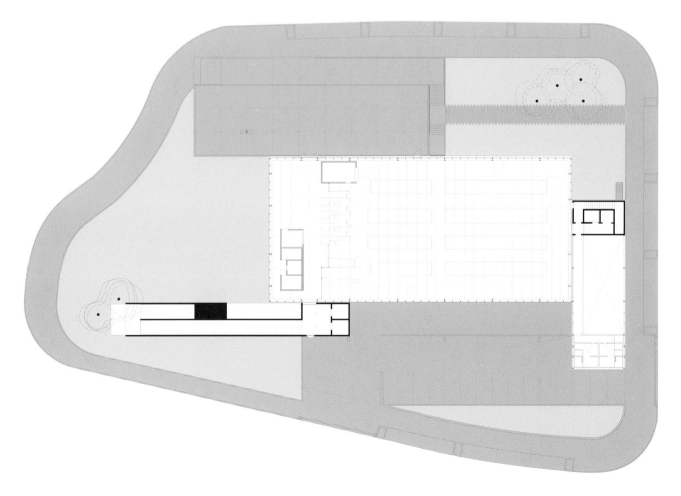

↑ | **Interior view**
↗ | **Main view**, with e-service station for bikes
→ | **Entrance,** mostly glazed

Öko-Billa

Perchtoldsdorf

A main focus of the Eco-Billa design is sustainability. The wood construction uses 53 percent less energy than a conventional store. The project was realized as part of a community project, involving the Rewe group and the Perchtoldsdorf community. This pioneering project was built within a time frame of just four months, and is characterized by energy and building technology that saves resources. Energy saving technology includes chill cabinets with doors, waste heat from the cooling units used for floor heating, predictive control, photovoltaic systems, e-service station for bikes and e-cars and LED lighting only. The entrance area is mostly glazed and the volume has been cleverly fitted into the site topography.

PROJECT FACTS
Address: Donauwörtherstraße 46–48, 2380 Perchtoldsdorf, Austria. **Client:** Rewe International AG.
Completion: 2011. **Gross floor area:** 1,000 m². **Estimated visitors:** 1,000 per day.

↑ | **Chill cabinets,** with doors
↙ | **Site plan**

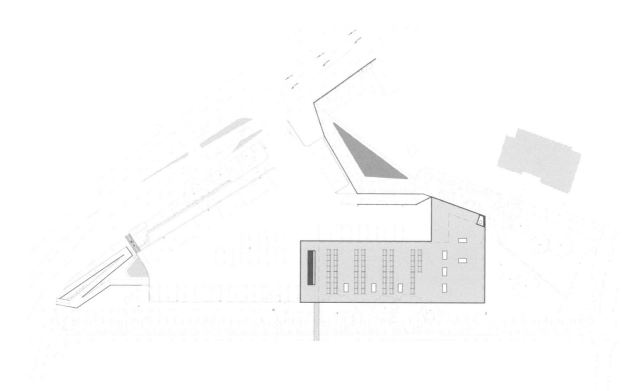

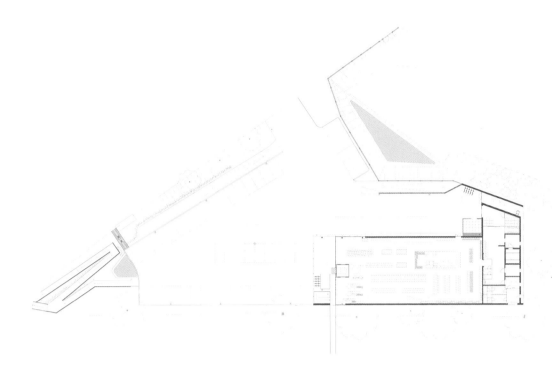

↑ | **Ground floor,** with parking lot
↓ | **Façade**

↑ | **View from east**
→ | **Site plan**

Soho Peaks

Beijing

The Soho Peaks building complex is a beacon along the way to Beijing's modern gateway, the Capital Airport, and the journey of transition to and from the city. Like Chinese fans, the two volumes appear to move around each other in an intricate dance, each embracing the other to from continuously changing angles. This interplay creates a vibrant architectural complex that is enhanced by an equally dynamic external skin, continuously varying to create a shimmering presence. The building is articulated into a major and minor volume, each embracing the other as two distinct forms that form a single design. Each volume houses office space, and the two are connected by a retail podium. This articulation helps to differentiate and loosen the building mass within the given site, boundary, and solar envelope constraints.

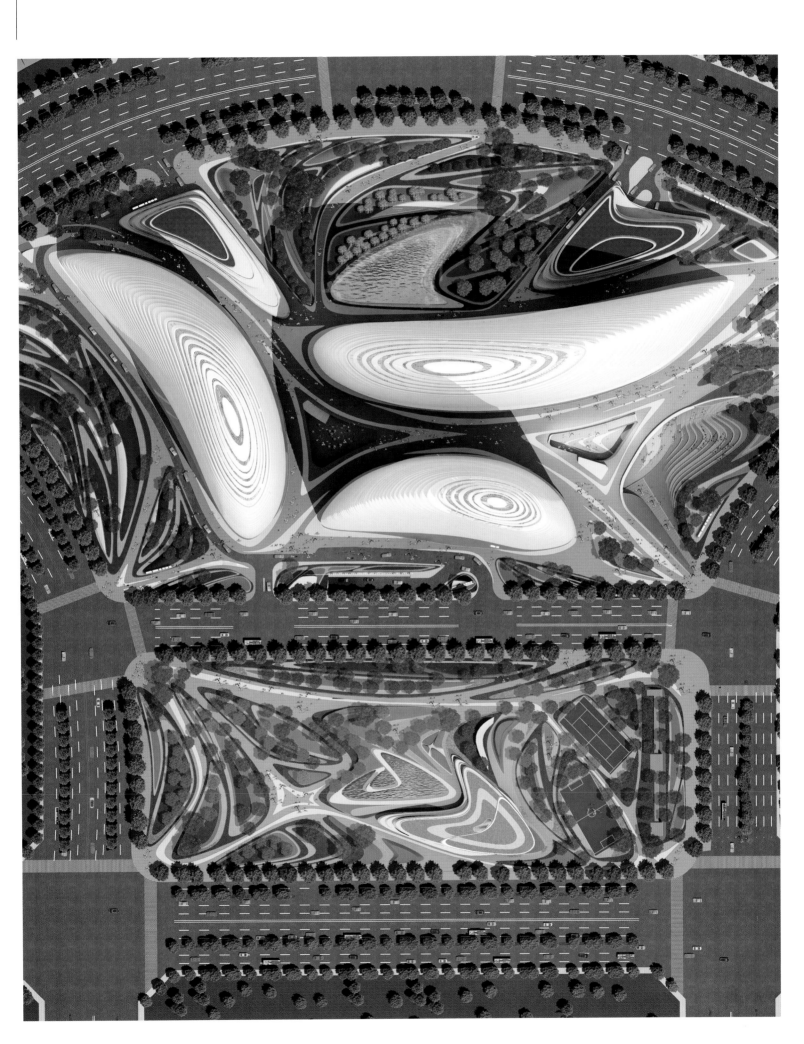

↑ | View from north
↓ | North elevation

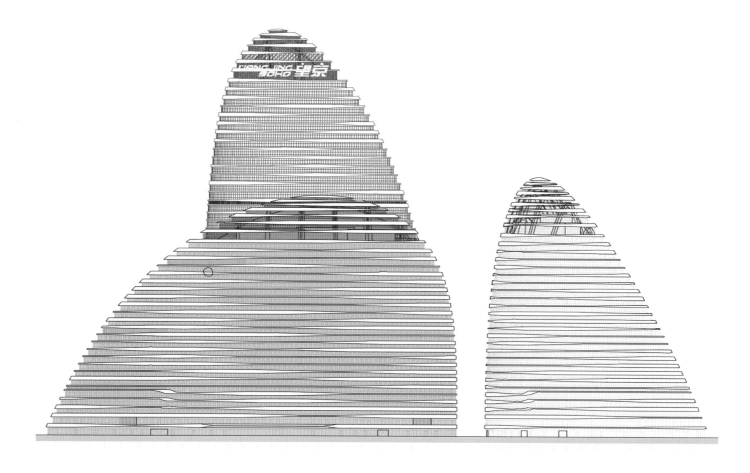

← | **Interior**, showroom
↓ | **Showroom**

↑ | **Market,** covers the main road
→ | **Roof,** creates a shaded functional and flexible space

Sant Antoni Sunday Market

Barcelona

The relocation of Sant Antoni Sunday Market required a site located near the old market, which is currently being refurbished. Hosting a weekly market, a temporary solution was needed that was both flexible and functional. These requirements led to the decision to cover Urgell Street, which is closed to traffic every Sunday. In order to safeguard the Sunday activity the architects covered the central area of the street with a light roof, supported by arcades on the sidewalks. The structure is four-and-a-half meters in height, respecting the height required for this type of urban road.

PROJECT FACTS

Address: Carrer Comte d'Urgell. Barcelona, Spain. **Client:** Institut Municipal de Mercats de Barcelona–Ajuntament de Barcelona. **Completion:** 2011. **Gross floor area:** 1,918 m².

↑ | **Main view**
← | **Side view**

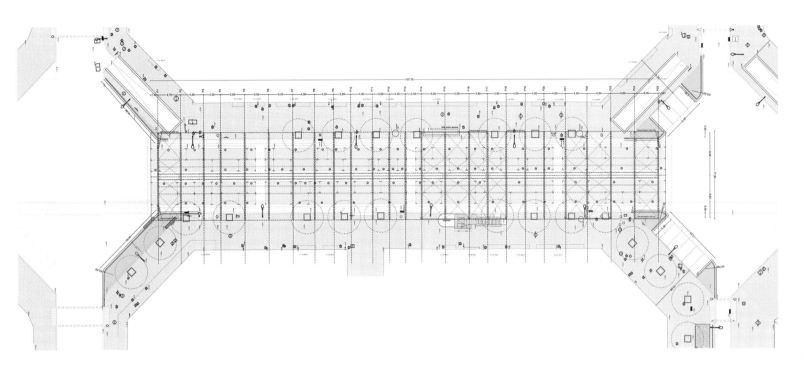

↑ | Layout plan
↓ | Market stall

Migdal Arquitectos/Jaime Varon, Abraham Metta, Alex Metta

↑ | **Restored area,** new gourmet restaurant zone
↗ | **Different shopping levels**
→ | **Canopy roof,** provides a weather-protected area

Town Center El Rosario

Mexico City

Town Center El Rosario is a shopping mall located in Azcapotzalco, north-east of Mexico city. The shopping center is vertically developed with three commercial and three basement levels. The space is governed by a central axis or atrium where the most important flows are developed. The shops and anchor stores are located around the atrium, with the particularity of having an anchor department store built right on top of another. Town Center El Rosario is one of a kind in Mexico. In addition to its blend of contemporary and 17th-century architecture.

PROJECT FACTS

Address: Avenida El Rosario 1025, Aquiles Serdan, Colonia El Rosario, 02100 Azcapotzalco, Mexico City, Mexico. **Client:** confidential. **Completion:** 2012. **Gross floor area:** 178,500 m². **Estimated visitors:** 30,000 per day. **Additional functions:** cinemas, lake, museum, park, skating rink, soccer field, sports center.

↑ | **Exterior view**, at night
← | **Restored area,** museum and dining

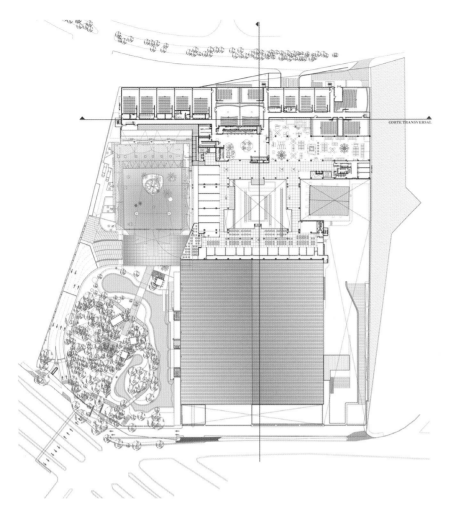

↖ | **Site plan**
↓ | **Interior,** glass roof ensures that plenty of light is drawn into the mall

Erick van Egeraat

↑ | **Exterior view**
↘ | **Building at dusk**

↗ | **Building in context**
→ | **Lighting at night**

Vershina Trade and Entertainment Center

Surgut

The Vershina Trade and Entertainment Center by Erik van Egeraat is an international shopping center, housing a wealth of retail, dance studios, restaurants, bars, an underground nightclub and extreme sports areas. The facility has something for everyone, regardless of age. The building design is based on an intricate play of light and shadow, opaque and transparent, open and closed. The incisions in the façade allow daylight to flow in during the day and artificial light to flow out at. These incisions also help to divide the solid building mass into smaller sections, giving it a dynamic and welcoming appearance.

PROJECT FACTS

Address: Intersection of Mir Avenue and General Ivanov Street, Surgut, Russia. **Client:** SKU Group.
Completion: 2010. **Gross floor area:** 37,000 m². **Additional functions:** dance studio, extreme sport arenas, underground, night club.

← | **Interior view,** from atrium upwards
↓ | **Section**

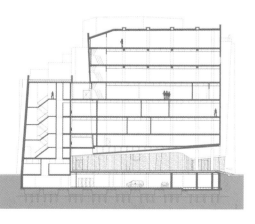

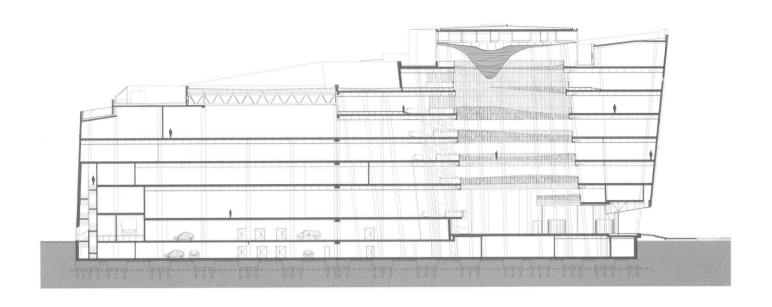

↑ | **Section**
↓ | **Interior**, atrium

↓ | **Interior**, different levels and lift

↑ | **Bird's-eye view**
→ | **South atrium,** silver and gray nuances with reflective textures

Hanjie Wanda Square

Wuhan

UNStudio's overall design for a new luxury shopping plaza in the Wuhan Central Culture Center was selected by Wanda as the winning entry for the façade and interior of the Hanjie Wanda Square. It will house international luxury brand stores, world-class boutiques, catering outlets and cinemas. The concept of luxury is incorporated by means of ideas focusing on craftsmanship of noble, yet simple materials. As water was utilized as a main organizational principle in the design for the Wuhan Central Cultural Center the theme 'synergy of flows' is used for the organization of the buildings. The interior concept is developed around the north and south atria, creating two different, yet integrated atmospheres. The façade design achieves a dynamic effect reflecting the handcrafted combination of two materials: polished stainless steel and alabaster.

PROJECT FACTS

Address: Wuhan, China. **Structural engineers:** Arup. **Landscape architects:** Loos van Vliet. **Client:** Wuhan Wanda East Lake Real State Co., Ltd. **Completion:** 2013. **Gross floor area:** 22,630 m². **Additional functions:** cinemas.

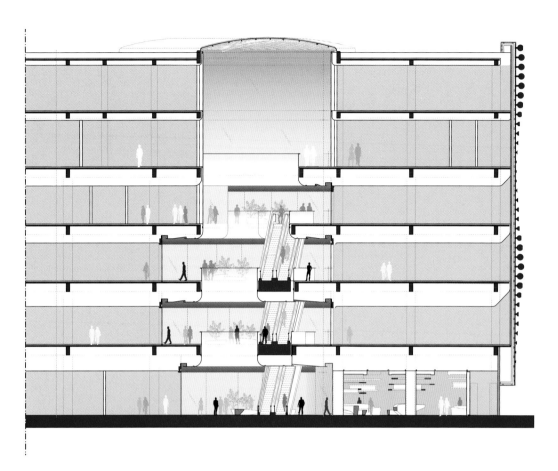

↑ | **Cross section**
← | **North atrium,** recognized as a main venue
hall

← | **North atrium,** characterized by warm golden and bronze materials
↓ | **Polished stainless steel and alabaster façade,** LED-lighting at night

GAD - Global Architectural
Development

↑ | Front view

A+ Shopping Center

Istanbul

The Ataköy Plus, called A+, Shopping Center is located in Atakoy, a district of Istanbul, Turkey. Atakoy Plus Shopping Center provides an alternative solution to the standard shopping experience, and offers a contemporary solution to a rapidly evolving building type in Istanbul. The building expresses its many functions through its complex façade, which, while providing a glimpse of the retail stores inside, serves as a constantly changing dynamic surface that also keeps up with the changes in its environment. The façade of the building performs as a layering of alternating surfaces, including a wire mesh skin wrapping the rigid steel and glass inner structure. The program is arranged to actively engage both the customers and retailers within, while also announcing itself to the community on the exterior as a unique and modern shopping experience.

PROJECT FACTS

Address: Ataköy Konakları, Adnan Kahveci Bulvarı, 6. Kısım, Ataköy-Istanbul, Turkey. **Completion:** 2010. **Gross floor area:** 25,000 m². **Additional functions:** children's play center, public park, terrace area.

↑ | Façade
↓ | Interior view

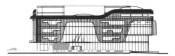

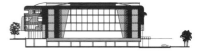

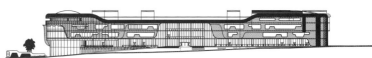

↑ | Elevation of façades

↑ | **Open plan interior,** with exposed structural systems
↗ | **Membrane screen,** protects the transparent volume below from overheating
→ | **Green design**

Jibi Markt

Hanover

This grocery store is an addition to a neighborhood where the concern for the environment has resulted in a range of both typological and architectural innovations. The client wanted the building to be a significant social and 'eco and archi-friendly' place. Roof photovoltaics and inside cooling components with closable lids add to the building's efficiency. Of the two volumes, the main volume is mainly covered with planted ivy, which acts as a thermal buffer, and partly with a green ceramic façade. The bioclimatic mesh membrane screen of the other volume acts as an urban loggia of mercantile significance.

Address: Mengendamm 3, 30177 Hanover, Germany. **Client:** Supermarkt Projektentwicklung GmbH & Co KG. **Completion:** 2009. **Gross floor area:** 2,400 m².

↑ | Ceramic green façade
← | Vegetative green façade

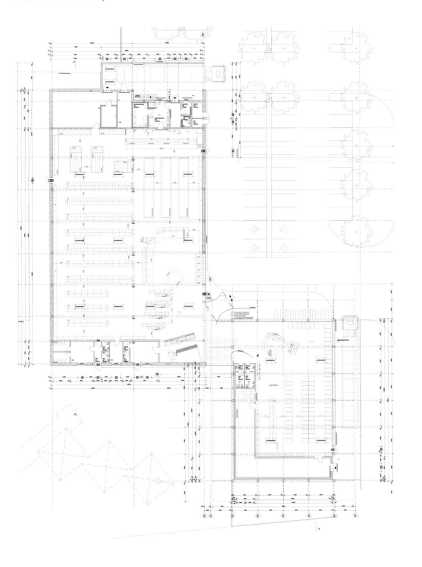

← | **Ground floor plan**
↓ | **Section**

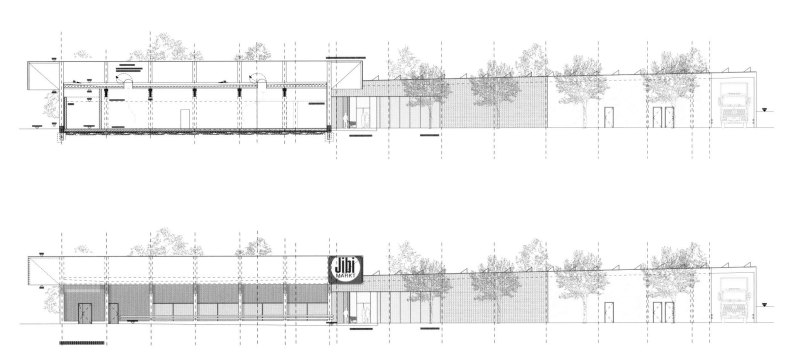

↑ | **View from the street,** at night
→ | **Terraces**

Cascade Commercial Center

Zagreb

Cascade Commercial Center is situated in the center of Zagreb, about 500 meters to the north of the main city square where the flat lowland part of Zagreb meets the elite housing-covered city hills. The architectural concept responds to the context. The building adapts to suit the topography; two terraces have been built between two parallel streets, each on a different elevation. As visitors walk along Tkalcica street, one of the important streets of Zagreb, the section of the building ensures visual contact with four streets in the center. They are filled with people sitting in cafés, shopping or just window shopping.

PROJECT FACTS

Address: Ulica Ivana Tkalcica 75A, 10000 Zagreb, Croatia. **Client:** Molteh d.o.o. **Completion:** 2009.
Gross floor area: 18,000 m². **Additional functions:** offices, residential.

↑ | **Terraces,** at night
← | **Apartments**

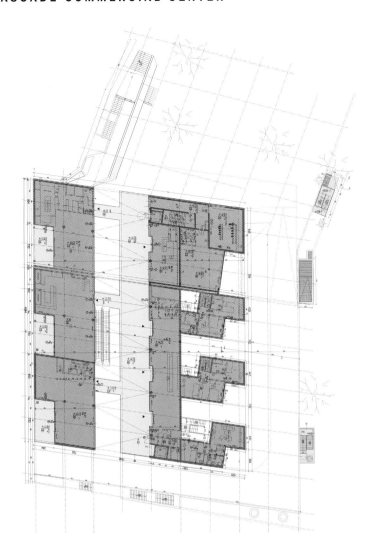

← | Ground floor plan
↓ | Section

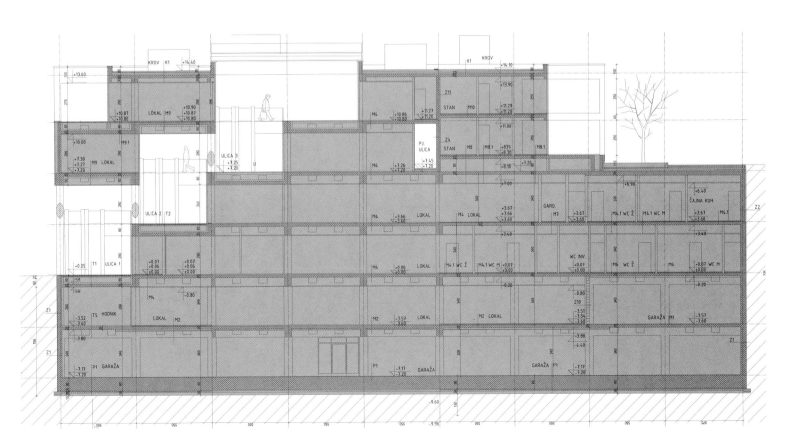

form A architekten

↑ | **Front view**
↓ | **Façade**, with timber slats
↘ | **Small-scale façade**
↘↘ | **Passersby gain insight and outlook**

↗ | **Façade**
→ | **Staircase**

Postplatz Forum

Waiblingen

The new development area on the "Alten Postplatz" is located at the interface between the historical Old Town, characterized by its medieval buildings, and the modern city development to the south. The goal of the planning phase was to redefine the transition from the Old Town to the modern urban development. The entire building volume looks like it is divided into separate houses, which lean slightly towards each other, similar to the arrangement of the houses in the historical old town. This creates a number of incisions in the main façade, which are closed with wither timber slats or doors. This gives the façade a unified yet small-scale appearance.

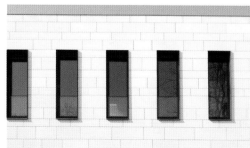

PROJECT FACTS

Address: Alter Postplatz 9–15, 71332 Waiblingen, Germany. **Client:** Matrix Immobilien AG. **Completion:** 2008. **Gross floor area:** 15,094 m². **Additional functions:** doctor's practice.

↑ | **Interface,** between historical Old Town and modern city development
← | **Fire escape**

← | Parking area
↓ | Site plan

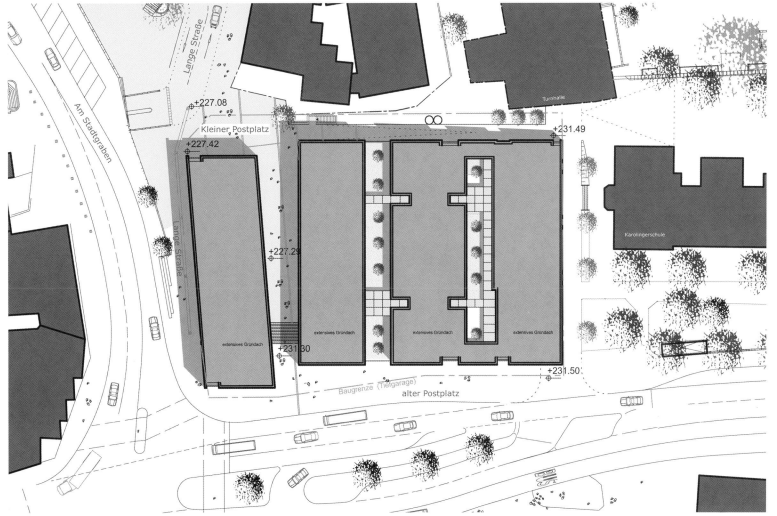

↑ | **Main view**, entrance

Wisma Atria

Singapore

The 2012 transformation of Wisma Atria is designed to further augment street visibility and respond to the patterns of human movement through the site. The materiality of the new façade is a dialogue between triangulated, faceted glass storefronts and a matte-aluminum finish for the cladding of structure and mechanical systems. The new stairs serve the double purpose of a permanent flood barrier and as a direct pedestrian link to the mall's new main entrances on the second story. The intention of the lighting design was to highlight the crystalline structure of the new façade in an elegant and timeless manner. The combined redevelopment measures for the mall have been conceived to strongly reposition the Wisma Atria mall in the increasingly competitive Orchard Road retail environment.

Address: 2 435 Orchard Road, 238877 Singapore, Singapore. **Original building:** 1986. **Client:** Aspinden Holdings Ltd. **Completion:** 2004. **Gross floor area:** 41,330 m².

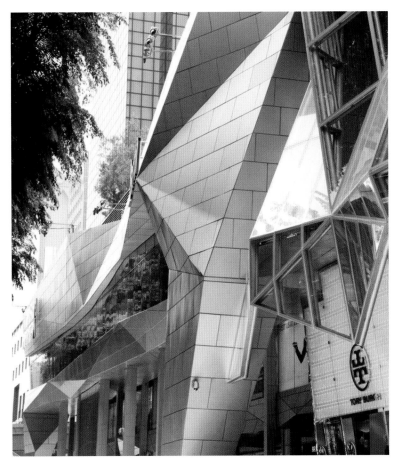

↑ | Matte aluminum finish
↓ | Glass façade

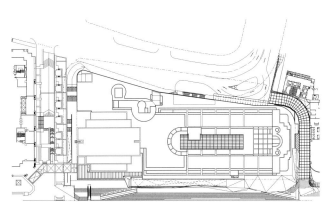

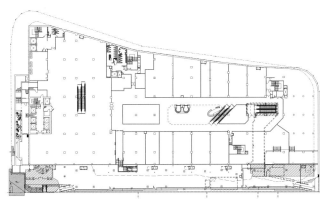

↑ | Site plan and first floor plan
↓ | Building, at night

↑ | **West façade**
↗ | **South façade**
→ | **South façade**, entrance at night

Riga Plaza

Riga

The idea behind this design was to integrate the functional requirements of the two-story shopping mall with a dynamic, long and flexible façade that is reminiscent of a belt. The 'active' surface of the façade responds to the dynamic surroundings – the 'Salu Tilts' bridge and a busy transport network – and can be easily identified from afar. The sinuous form of the façade was inspired by the Daugava River, which runs along the entire country as a long ribbon. The dynamic character of the building is accentuated by the use of multicolored metallic sheets. The selected colors – gray, white, light blue and black – come from native costume motifs.

PROJECT FACTS

Address: Mukusalas street 71, Riga, 1004 Latvia. **Interior designers:** Buki Zucker designers & architects. **Client:** confidential. **Completion:** 2009. **Gross floor area:** 89,968 m². **Estimated visitors:** 12,000 per day. **Additional functions:** cinema, offices.

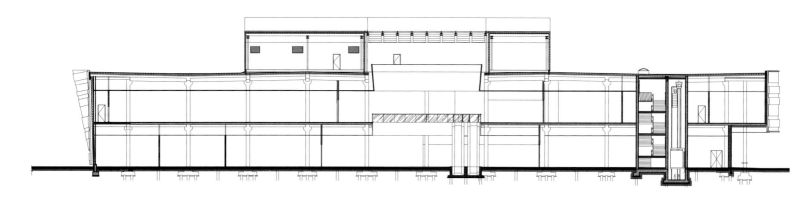

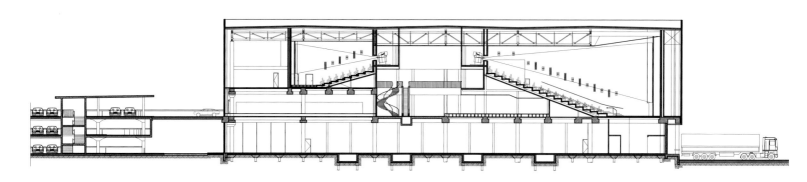

↑ | **Sections**
← | **Interior,** commercial gallery

← | **Interior,** shopping street
↓ | **Ground floor plan**

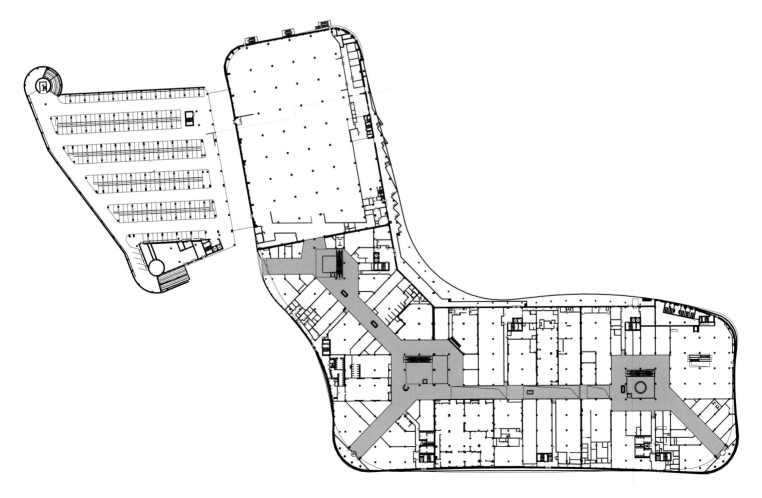

↑ | **Front view,** during opening
↗ | **Façade**
→ | **Retail unit**

Mini Mall

Rotterdam

The Mini Mall comprises 2,600 square meters of retail and catering space for entrepreneurs, artists, designers and other creative minds, who will breathe new life into this unique area. The development of the Hofplein Station into a compact shopping mall comes in response to a lack of affordable locations in Rotterdam where fresh new initiatives can see the light of day, but also with the aim of improving the quality of the neighborhood. The Mini Mall offers space for special catering outlets, original shop formats for independent designers, vintage clothing, high class sneakers, handmade accessories, comics and second-hand furniture.

PROJECT FACTS

Address: Raampoortstraat 30, 3032 AH Rotterdam, The Netherlands. **Original building:** A. van Hemert, 1907. **Client:** Hofbogen BV. **Completion:** 2011. **Gross floor area:** 2,600 m². **Estimated visitors:** 150 per day. **Additional functions:** roof top event space.

↑ | **Exterior view**
← | **Event space,** on roof

← | Restaurant
↓ | Elevation and sections

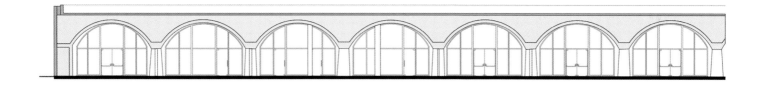

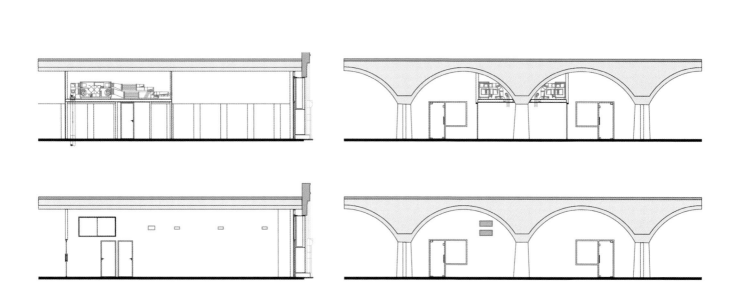

↑ | **Front view**
↗ | **Bright colors and big windows**
→ | **Interior view**

Bavier-Center

Erkrath

The former Hertie department store on this site dated back to 1973. This mall design concept by pos4, working in close collaboration with the Hahn Group, has given the inner city area a new lease of life. The building has been integrated into the architectural fabric and the building's 1970s architecture has been reinterpreted. One successful aspect of the revitalization is the perfect scale of the shopping center. Three new elevators, a new entrance solution, and uninterrupted views of the inner-city increase the value of both the location and the property. The original relief panels have been maintained and reworked with modern windows, bringing the building out of the past and placing it firmly in the present.

PROJECT FACTS

Address: Bavierstraße 10, 40699 Erkrath, Germany. **Original building:** 1973. **Client:** Hahn FMZ Erkrath GmbH & Co.KG. **Completion:** 2010. **Gross floor area:** 13,300 m². **Estimated visitors:** 4,000 per day.

Am Weinb

Auf dem Sand   Schöne Aussicht
       Galileistraße
Am Maiblümchen

↑ | Street names decorate the walls
↙ | Ground floor plan

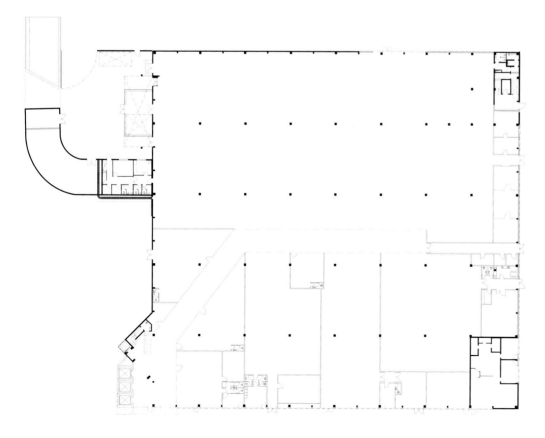

← | Bright interior
↑ | Original building
↓ | Entrance, signal color

↑ | Illuminated façade
↗ | Radial façade
→ | Two symmetrical volumes

Sokol City Shopping & Business Center

St. Petersburg

This building is a composition of two vertical equal volumes on a developed stylobate, which functions as an entrance level. In the stylobate are a shopping center and the entry lobby of a business center. The radical façades of the office buildings open out to Komendantsky prospekt, while the symmetrical planes of the rear façades form the center of Bogatyrsky prospekt and prospekt Sizova. The axis of Komendantsky prospekt is perceived as a gap between vertical spaces through their entire height. On the top of the stylobate, it is proposed to place a square where city residents, employees and visitors of the complex can relax. The main shape-forming details of the façade are the tiered overhanging sections of the floors.

PROJECT FACTS

Address: Bogatyrsky prospekt 32, Primorsky adm. district, St. Petersburg 190000, Russia. **Client:** OOO Femida. **Completion:** ongoing. **Gross floor area:** 132,535 m². **Estimated visitors:** 10,000 per day. **Additional functions:** offices.

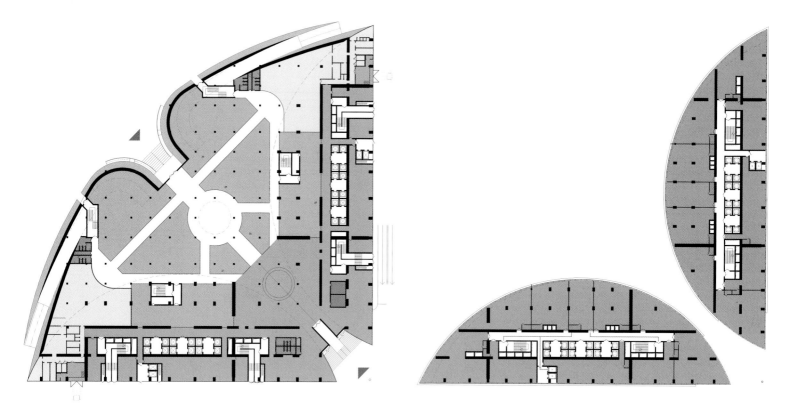

↑ | First floor plan
← | Bird's-eye view

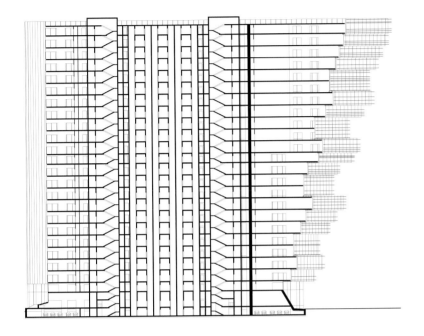

← | Section
↙ | Ground floor plan
↓ | Façade

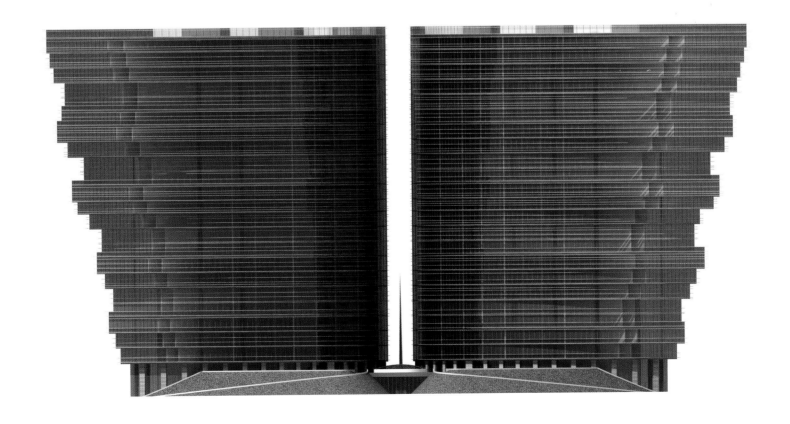

↑ | **Exterior view**, entrance area
↓ | **Section**

→ | **Interior view**

Boulevard Berlin

Berlin

Schlossstraße in Berlin's Steglitz district is one of the most important shopping streets in Berlin. The former premises of the Wertheim and Karstadt department stores have been renovated and joined together to form a new shopping center: the Berlin Boulevard now forms its own small shopping quarter. Centrally positioned along Schlossstraße, the complex comprises a number of different building elements connected by passages and open squares that give the public space a new character.

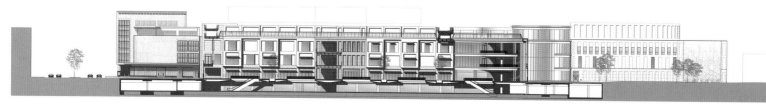

Address: Schloßstraße 10, 12163 Berlin, Germany. **Client:** Multi Development Germany, Multi Veste Berlin GmbH. **Completion:** 2012. **Gross floor area:** 182,000 m².

↑ | **Shopping street**
← | **Rear,** with garden

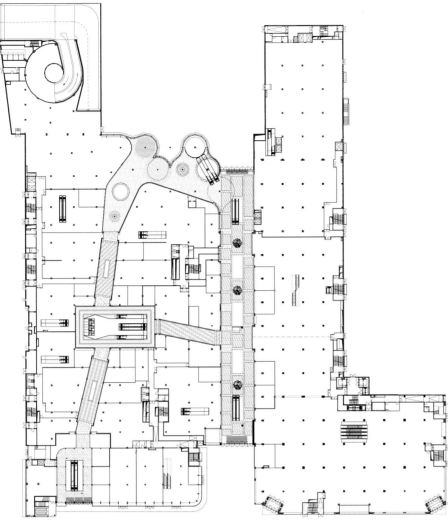

← | **Ground floor plan**
↓ | **Exterior view,** sinuous design

↑ | **Master plan**
→ | **Cityscape**

Danzishi Retail and Entertainment District

Chongqing

COMPRISING a total of 800,000 square meters of accommodation, this development includes 150,000 square meters of dedicated high-end retail and entertainment areas. Working within the parameters of local planning constraints, the design aims to provide a cohesive solution that is both pragmatic and architecturally innovative within the context. By creating a series of terraced retail courtyards surrounding sheltered garden plazas and linked together by elevated walkways, the 14 plots are connected by common features whilst allowing for distinct architectural languages to differentiate their respective identities.

PROJECT FACTS

Address: New Central Business District in Danzishi, Chongqing, China. **Client:** Chongqing Planning Bureau, Chongqing Energy Investment Group, NVC-Lighting Technology Corporation, Sinosteel Investment Group, Zhongxun Group. **Completion:** 2016. **Gross floor area:** 800,000 m². **Estimated visitors:** 200,000 per day. **Additional functions:** hotel, offices, residential.

↑ | **Retail street frontage**
← | **Sinosteel buildings,** landscaped retail courtyard

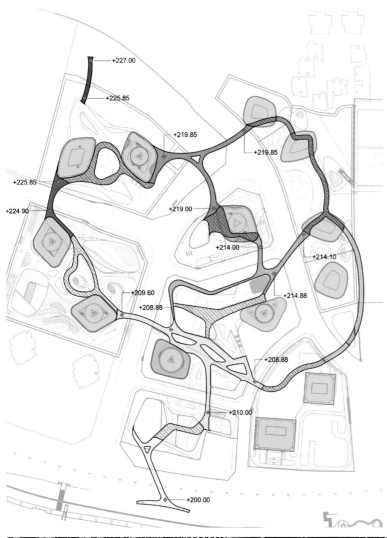

+227.00
+225.85
+219.85
+219.85
+225.85
+224.90
+219.00
+214.00
+214.10
+209.60
+214.88
+208.88
+208.88
+210.00
+200.00

← | Retail circulation loop
↓ | NVC lighting towers one and two,
terraced retail deck

↑ | **Front façade**
↗ | **Bird's-eye view**
→ | **Sketch, bird's-eye view**

Siófok Pláza

Siófok

Already more than 200 years old, Siófok is the capital city of Lake Balaton in Hungary. The architects planned the Siófok Pláza in the middle of the main square in the developing downtown area. The modern 21st-century building is situated between two historical symbols; the Water Tower (1912), and the Pub (1895). The architects' intention was to plan a building that communicates with the surrounding historical city center. The design features a transparent glass façade towards the main square of the city, with a cobweb-like metal screen. The building of the old pub is integrated into the new building by the inner shopping arcade.

PROJECT FACTS

Address: Szabadság tér 6, 8600, Siófok, Hungary. **Structural engineers:** Konstruaterv. **Landscape architects:** Pm Garden. **Client:** Sio Invest Kft. **Completion:** 2012. **Gross floor area:** 18,594 m². **Estimated visitors:** 4,500 per day. **Additional functions:** bowling, cinema.

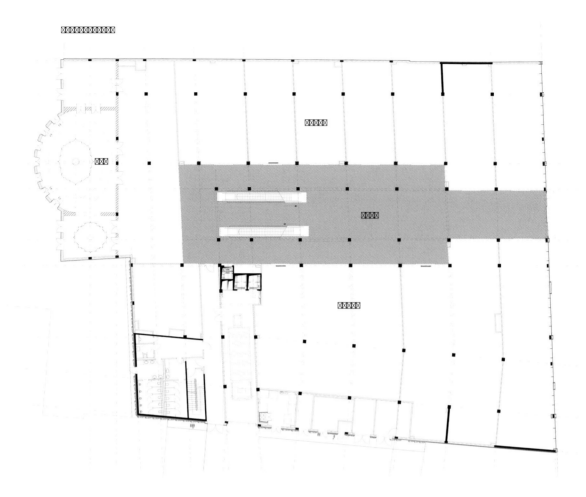

↑ | Ground floor plan
← | The old pub

← | Interior view
↓ | Second floor plan

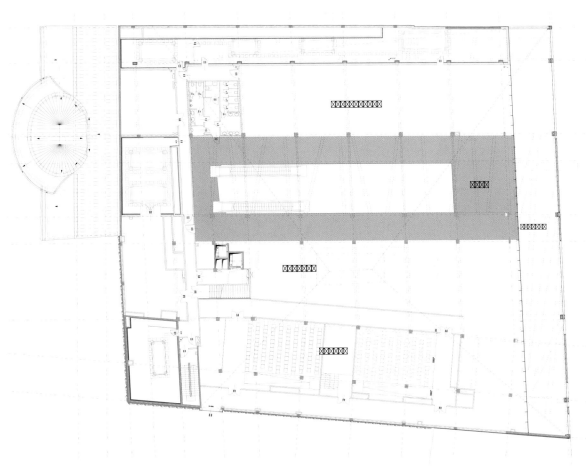

↑ | **North façade**
↗ | **Central court**
→ | **Main entrance**

Vivaci

Guarda

This small shopping center in the city of Guarda, Portugal, is located on the boundary between its historical core and the 1950s urban prompansion. Bridging a grade level difference of 20 meters between the bordering streets, the mall houses five levels of retail and three levels of parking. Inside, the open void evolves to form a revolving crescendo in conjunction with the position of the escalators, culminating in a large hexagonal skylight designed in a kaleidoscopic combination of terrazzo color stripes identifying each level. The façade is an abstraction of the geological metaphor of the slope, with the layers of the floor levels presented as zigzagging panels of white precast concrete elements, interrupted by fissures of colored glass.

PROJECT FACTS

Address: Avenida dos Bombeiros Voluntários Egitanienses 5, 6300-523 Guarda, Portugal. **Client:** FDO Imobiliária, SA. **Completion:** 2008. **Gross floor area:** 21,900 m².

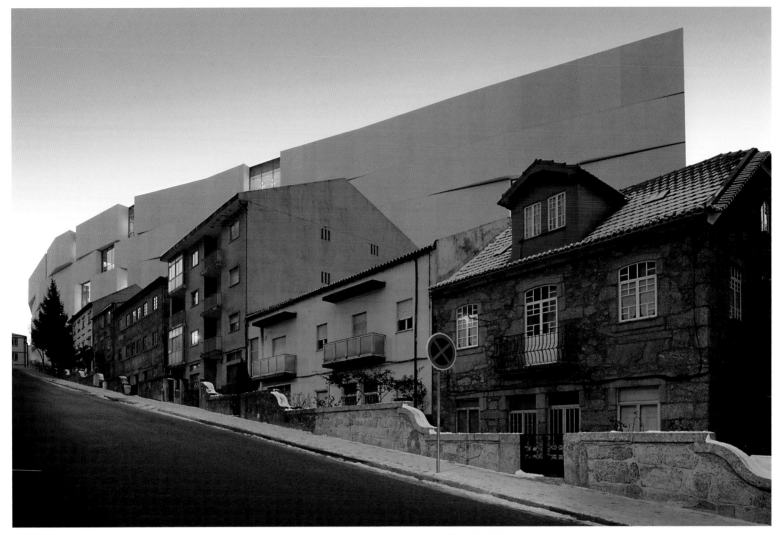

↑ | **Historical setting**
← | **Interior view**

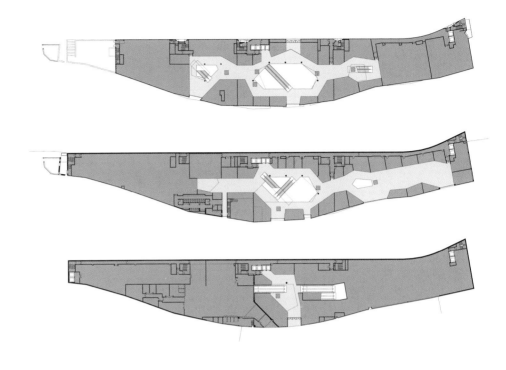

↑ | Floor plans
↙ | Section
↓ | Plans of the façade

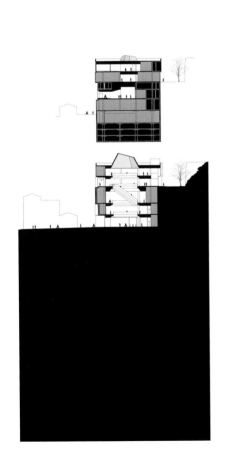

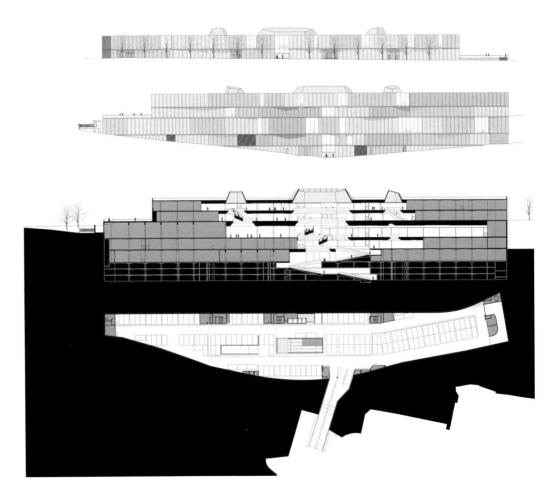

↑ | Ice rink
↗ | View from the rear
→ | Interior view

Wutzky

Berlin

Originally opened in 1968 as Ladenzentrum Süd, Wutzky was once Berlin's largest shopping center within a closed housing estate. Between 2011 and 2012, the open and often drafty shopping mall was modernized and expanded by degewo, Berlin's leading housing corporation. As part of the renewal and expansion, Wutzky now has direct access to the Wutzkyallee metro station. Two restaurants and a café open the shopping center out towards Rotraut-Richter-Platz, giving the area a new flair. The complex also houses a 800-square meter, barrier free medical center. Today, Wutzky is not only a modern and attractive shopping mall but also a vital community facility in southern Gropiusstadt.

Address: Joachim-Gottschalk-Weg 21, 12353 Berlin, Germany. **Original building:** Hans Bandel, 1968.
Landscape architects: Lützow 7 Cornelia Müller Jan Wehberg Garten- und Landschaftsarchitekten.
Client: degewo AG. **Completion:** 2012. **Gross floor area:** 35,675 m². **Additional functions:** eight medical
practices, degewo service center.

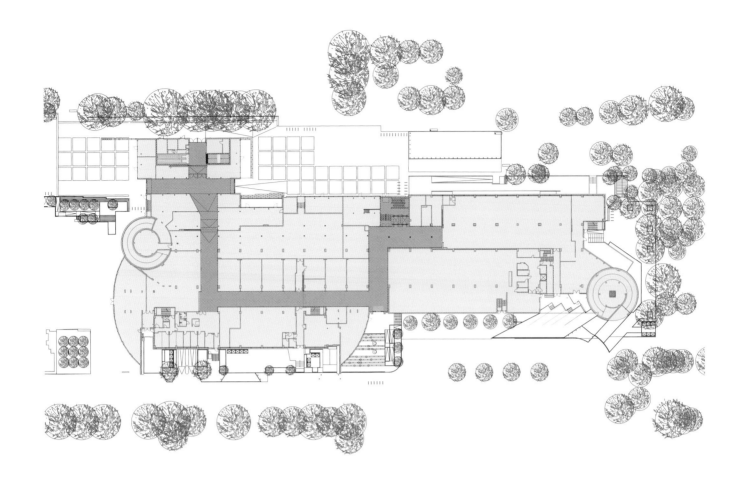

↑ | **Ground floor plan**
← | **Exterior view,** market stalls

← | **Shopping area**
↑ | **View before modernization**
↓ | **Bird's-eye view**, rendering

↑ | Exterior
→ | Interior atrium

Liverpool Department Store

Huixquilucan

Rojkind Arquitectos was commissioned to design a façade for this new department store. Located in the northern "car dependent" suburb of Interlomas on the outskirts of Mexico City, this relatively new suburb is characterized by a lack of open public space and a myriad of roads on which pedestrians are not welcome. The new façade responds to the fast pace of everyday life in this isolated suburb. The double-layered façade shelters the store and its users from its chaotic environment. The curved backlit balconies are intended as a reminder of the fluidity of the exterior façade. This play between inside and outside is intended to create a sense of discovery for the user that culminates with the roof garden. The roof terrace offers a park-like setting that can be enjoyed not only by the store visitors but also by the surrounding local community.

PROJECT FACTS

Address: Vialidad de la Barranca 6, Colonia Exhacienda Jesús del Monte, 52787 Huixquilucan, Mexico.
Client: Distribuidora Liverpool SA de CV. **Completion:** 2010. **Gross floor area:** 18,000 m². **Additional functions:** gourmet area on rooftop with park.

↑ | Interior development
← | Diagram

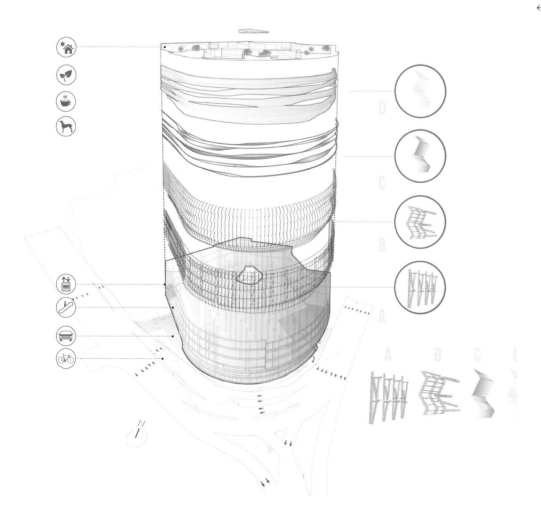

← | Façade detail
↓ | Bird's-eye view

↑ | **Historical portal,** incorporated into new façade
→ | **Entrance,** at night

Dot Envelope

Ljubljana

This site is listed as an historical industrial area and houses the buildings of an old butchery complex, including a water tower and an old butcher's hall. National Heritage demanded that the tower be rebuilt in its original state and that the main façade portal of the old hall be incorporated into the front of the planned new shopping mall. The proposed pattern was based on different stepped elevations in order to break down the basic cube shell. The surface needed for one side was then calculated. Within the budget constraints, the decision was made to use basic metal sheets. After another cost evaluation, it was determined that only 20 percent of the concrete shell could be covered with these metal sheets. In response, the sheets were perforated with holes in different sizes. The metal cut offs from these sheets were used and arranged on the rest of the façade.

PROJECT FACTS

Address: Mesarska cesta 11, 1000 Ljubljana, Slovenia. **Client:** Gradis G. Group, Mercator d.d.
Completion: 2008. **Gross floor area:** 2,800 m². **Estimated visitors:** 400 per day.

← | Perforated metal sheet and concrete façade sections
↓ | Section

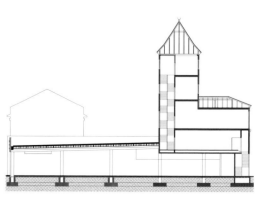

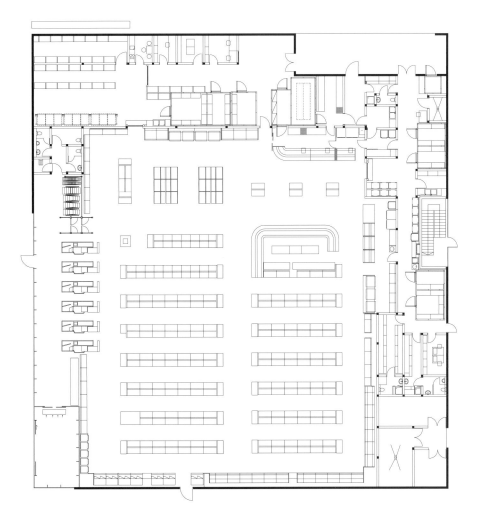

↖ | Ground floor plan
↓ | Façade detail

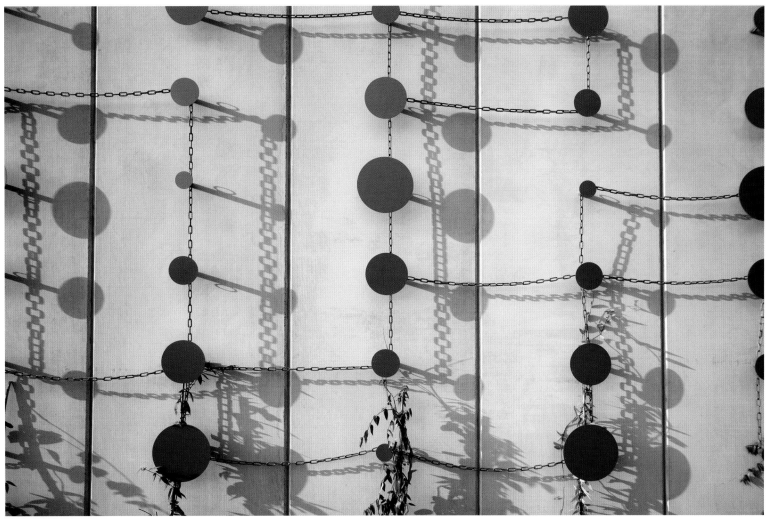

↑ | **Center court event plaza and 'green' wall feature,** night view
→ | **Day view**

Konoha Mall

Hashimoto

The new Konoha Mall represents a new 'eco-leisure' destination that introduces sustainability and eco-design principles into retail to create a compelling sense of place and experience. Inspired by its natural surroundings and the cultural influences of Hashimoto, Konoha Mall is an innovative retail solution that embraces nature and sustainability, along with fundamental retail strategies. Comprising 84,000 square meters of retail leisure functions, including 120 specialty shops and restaurants, a large community market anchor, and premier food court.

PROJECT FACTS

Address: 2-27-2 Hashimoto, Nishi-ku, Fukuoka, 819-0031, Japan. **Client:** Fukuoka Jisho Co., Ltd.
Completion: 2011. **Gross floor area:** 84,000 m². **Estimated visitors:** 14,000 per day. **Additional functions:** plazas, open space.

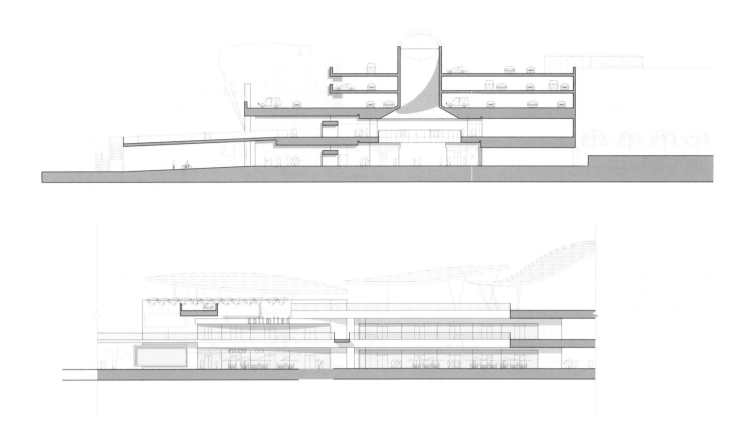

↑ | Sections
← | Nature-inspired center court

← | Open-air 'garden walk' district and landscape
↓ | Ground floor plan

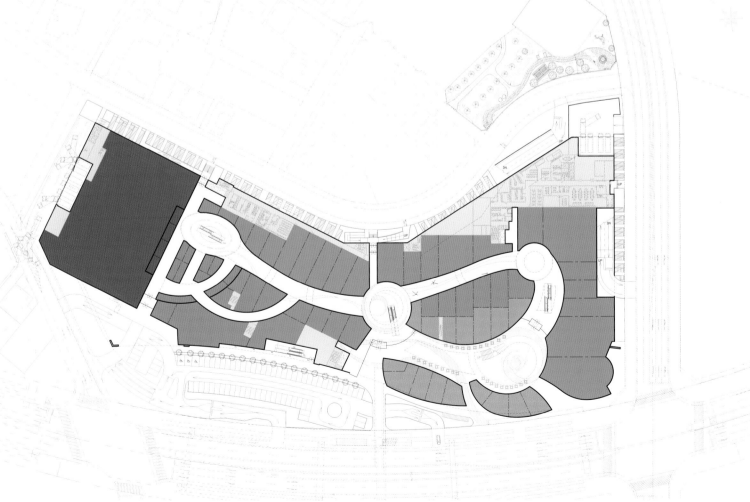

C.F. Møller Architects

↑ | **Interior street,** and new skylights

Glostrup Centre Renovation

Glostrup

The new façade concept for the Glostrup Centre is part of the renovation of a 1970s shopping center, close to Copenhagen. The project included the extension of the floor area and the interior spaces by raising the roof to double-story height above the central thoroughfare, as well as establishing extensive new skylights. The new façade forms a sculptural landmark, with new iconic entrances in flowing, organically curved shapes and a façade cladding of lateral strips of polycarbonate panels of varying transparency, balanced to match the underlying functions, allowing, for example, the café to receive daylight through the cladding. In the evenings the façade is back-lit by colored LEDs, dynamically programmed in different sequences to create an ever-changing appearance.

PROJECT FACTS

Address: Hovedvejen, 2600 Glostrup, Denmark. **Original building:** 1972. **Client:** Steen & Strøm Danmark A/S. **Completion:** 2010. **Gross floor area:** 37,000 m². **Estimated visitors:** 10,000 per day.

↑ | **Illuminated façade,** at night
↓ | **Plan**

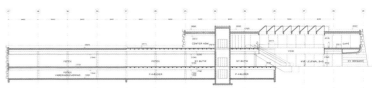

↑↑ | **Sketch**
↑ | **Section**
↓ | **Interior lobby,** with new skylights

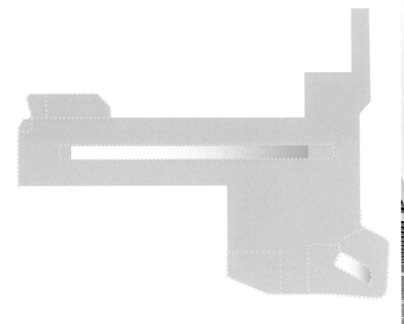

NEW FACADES

NEW SKYLIGHTS

↑ | **Escalators**
→ | **Interior view**

Markthalle

Basel

This market hall has been opened out and is now more freely accessible and appeals to the wider public. The entrance on Viaduktstrasse has been laid open – a large cascading staircase now provides access to the domed hall, strengthening the relationship to the main train station and giving the market hall an appearance more fitting to its urban environment. The area beneath the dome can be used to host a variety of events, ranging from private to community and commercial. Small-scale dining, sales and services areas are positioned around the event space. The utilization concept is completed with large retail stores in the basement level.

PROJECT FACTS

Address: Corner of Steintorberg, Innere Margarethenstrasse, Viaduktstrasse, 4051 Basel, Switzerland. **Original building:** H.E. Ryhiner, 1929. **Client:** Allreal AG, Credit Suisse Anlagestiftung. **Completion:** 2012. **Gross floor area:** 25,942 m². **Additional functions:** event space.

↑ | **Front view**
↓ | **Section**

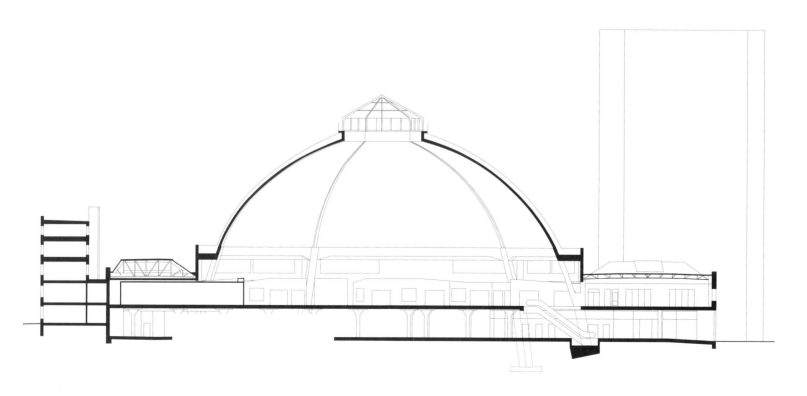

← | **Exterior view**
↓ | **Floor plan**, dome platform

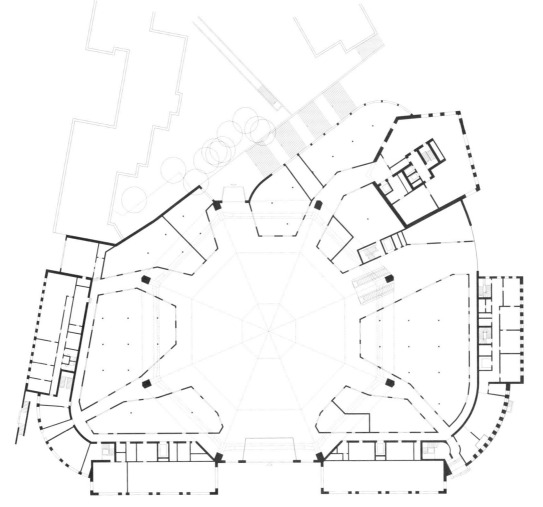

↑ | **Extension,** positions the center as a high fashion landmark

→ | **Revamped center,** offers more space and attractions for visitors

Chadstone West Mall

Chadstone

This expansion to Melbourne's Chadstone Centre creates one of the largest regional shopping centers in all of Australia. The center, one of the region's highest revenue-producing retail properties, has grown into an award-winning regional retail facility. The initial phase adds a new two-level high fashion district at the southern end of the center. Refined landscaping and bronze/stone detailing provides a new landmark identity and front door. Inside, the space is defined by a distinctive spiral of glass that culminates in seashell-shaped skylights. The second phase adds a new entertainment zone at the center's northern end. A new entry affords direct access to cinemas, restaurants and other entertainment venues. The existing eight-screen cinema is revamped and expanded to 19 screens on two levels. Two new parking structures complete the expansion.

PROJECT FACTS

Address: 1341 Dandenong Road, Chadstone 3148, Australia. **Client:** The Gandel Group of Companies.
Completion: 2009. **Gross floor area:** 43,014 m². **Additional functions:** cinema.

↑ | **Detailing and glass spiral,** culminating in skylights
← | **Expansive skylight,** offers exterior views and draws in natural light

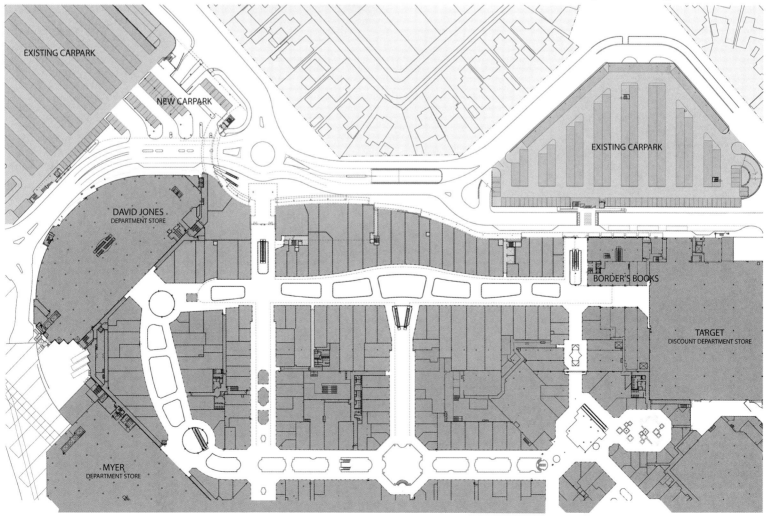

← | Retail area
↓ | Site and ground floor plan

↑ | **Entrance**
↓ | **Soft colors,** used to generate waves of colored light across the façade

→ | **Main atrium**

Galleria Centercity

Cheonan

The Galleria Cheonan department store marks the entrance to a new development area. Moiré effects, special lighting and animations ensure that the outside appearance changes constantly. Inside and outside are brought together in an intricate manner, as four different thematic interior clusters can be identified in the exterior surface. The repetition of curves, enhanced by coiled strip lighting in the ceilings of the platforms, gives the interior its distinctive character. The ceiling lighting produces a chandelier effect. There are three different spaces: the VIP Room, the art center, and the customer service areas.

PROJECT FACTS

Address: 521-3 Buldangdong, Seobukgu, Cheonan, South Korea. **Structural engineers:** Kopeg Engineering. **Lighting designers:** ag Licht, Bonn. **Landscape architects:** GANSAM Architects & Partners, Seoul. **Client:** Hanwha Galleria. **Completion:** 2010. **Gross floor area:** 66,700 m². **Additional functions:** art center and cultural center, cinema, roof terrace, VIP room.

← | **Different plateaus**
↓ | **Section**

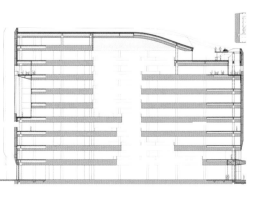

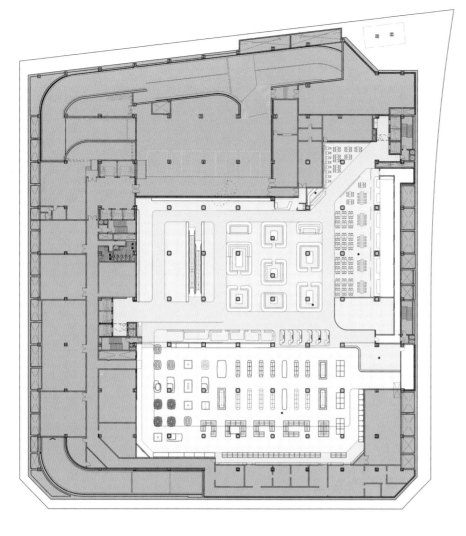

← | **Ground floor plan**
↙↓ | **Specially designed fixtures,** integrated within the mullions of the outer façade layer

↑ | **Main view**
→ | **Façade detail**

Liverpool Altabrisa

Villahermosa

Located in a strategic area at the south end of the city, the shopping center Liverpool Altabrisa is part of a new development pole for Villahermosa. The challenge presented by this project was the need to find a simple and effective construction system that would accelerate the production, assembly and installation of the façade, while at the same time, provide a complex and interesting proposal. The façade was built by combining five different types of precast concrete elements shaped like a propeller. Each of the propellers rotates 180 degrees on its axis and vary in height from 16 to 20 meters, depending on their position. This design gives the building a sense of movement.

PROJECT FACTS

Address: Plaza Villahermosa, 86179 Villahermosa, Mexico. **Interior designers:** FRCH design worldwide. **Client:** Liverpool. **Completion:** 2012. **Gross floor area:** 25,000 m².

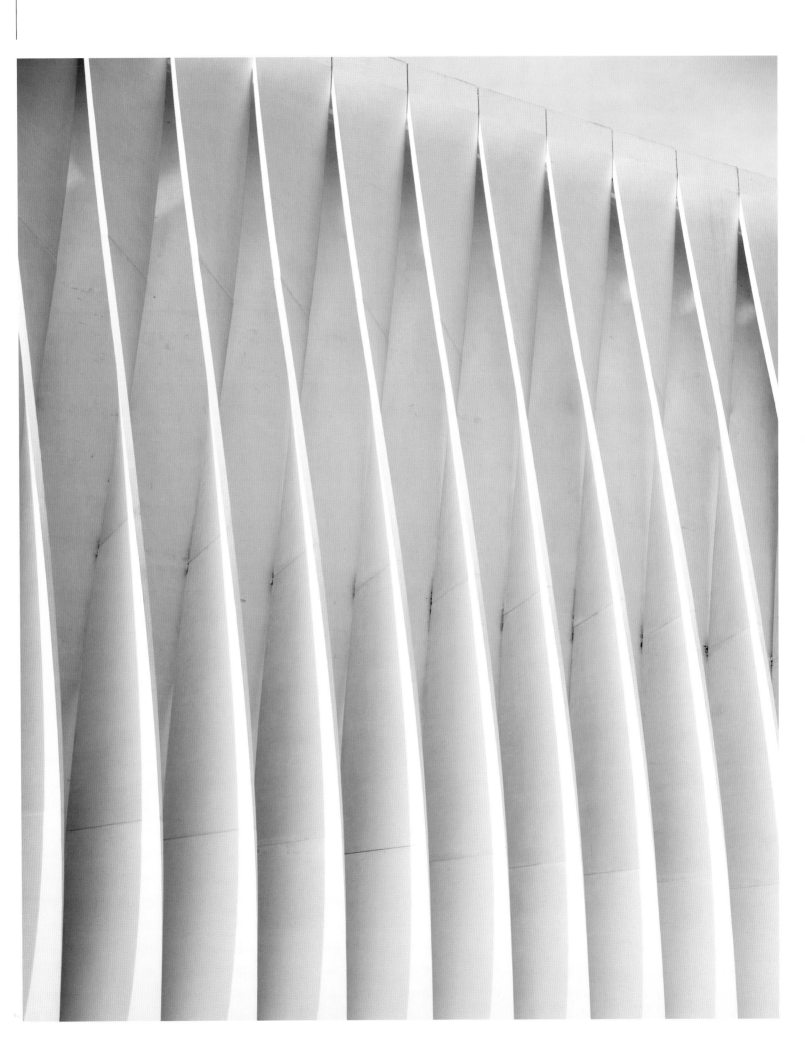

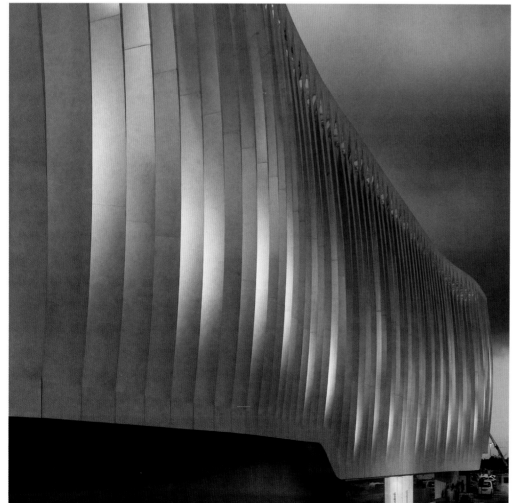

↑ | **Façade detail**
← | **Illuminated façade,** at night

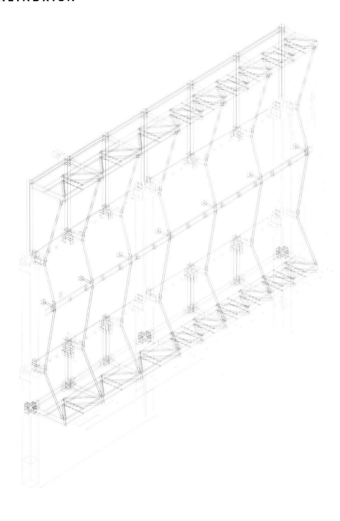

↖ | **Diagram**
↓ | **Building,** shines out like a beacon at night

↑ | **Main view**, lake with boats
↗ | **View of the lake**
→ | **Ice rink**, canal in summer

Puerto Venecia

Zaragoza

Located in an exceptional position and well connected with the city center and main transport arteries, Puerto Venecia offers a new concept in the world of big commercial areas, the shopping resort, based on the creation of spaces promoting a lasting experience for visitors. The resort is organized around a 500-meter linear park, with water as the main feature, bringing together a great range of activities including commercial, leisure, tourism and adventure for all ages. From a commercial point of view, this ambitious large-scale project should be seen as a supra-regional center. It combines various distinct elements, especially with its layout around a lake and green areas planted with a broad range of species.

PROJECT FACTS

Address: Travesía Jardines Reales nº 7, 50021 Zaragoza, Spain. **Landscape architects:** Mike Smith.
Lighting designers: Theo Kondos. **Client:** Eurofund Investments Zaragoza. **Completion:** 2012. **Gross
floor area:** 275,000 m². **Estimated visitors:** 50,000 per day. **Additional functions:** cinemas, leisure.

↑ | **Playing area,** by night
↙ | **Site plan**
↓ | **Elevation**

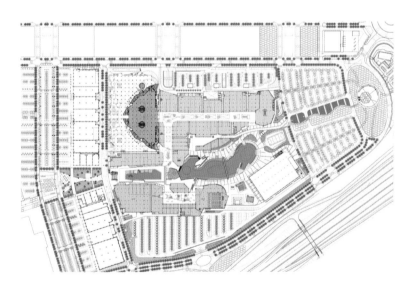

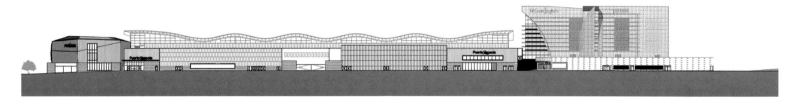

← | Shopping gallery
↓ | Seating area

↑ | **Urban super wall,** created with stacked LED blocks
↗ | **Aerial view**
→ | **Public plaza,** animated with LED façades

Summer International Shopping Mall

Zhuhai

This mall comprises 360,000 square meters of leasable retail space within a mixed commercial development totaling 510,000 square meters. The 'super wall' design comprises a series of giant, stacked stone, steel and LED blocks that open and cantilever out across the street. Within the wall, softer planted terrace building and street forms are revealed, like a giant 'secret garden'. The retail and entertainment hubs are organized around this public space, linking the external spaces. The hubs are further linked via internal bridges, providing a seamless, connected retail experience.

PROJECT FACTS

Address: Intersection of Cui Wei Dong Road and San Tai Shi Road, Qianshan, Zhuhai, China. **Interior designers:** 10+paringonions. **Client:** Summer Industry Group. **Completion:** 2015. **Gross floor area:** 510,000 m². **Estimated visitors:** 100,000 per day. **Additional functions:** cinema, hotel, kids and game zones, office, plaza.

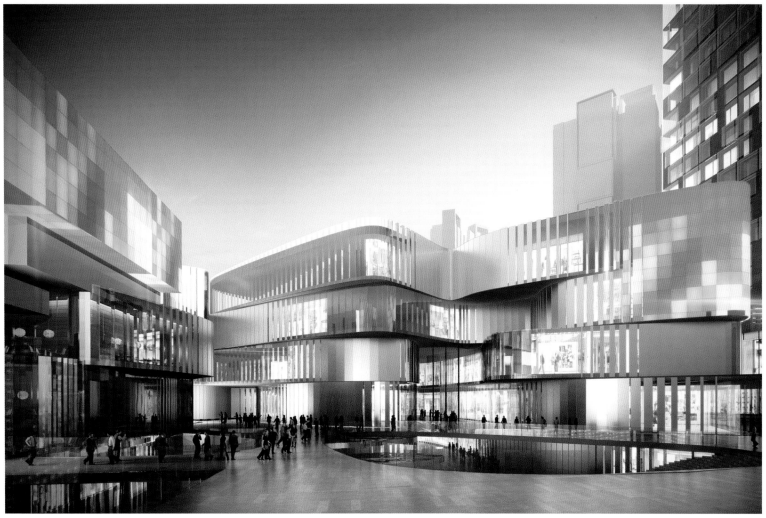

↑ | **'Secret Garden'**, shaded by a series of canopies
← | **Retail zones**

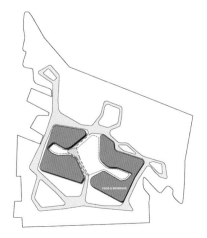

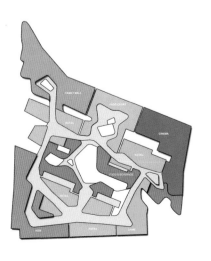

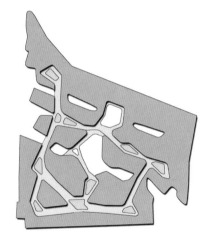

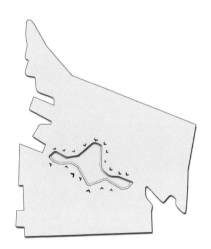

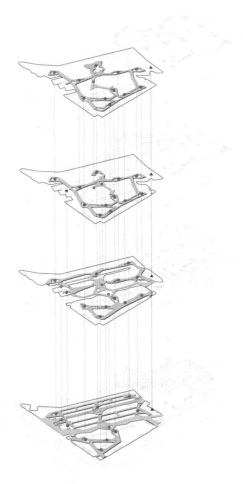

↖ | Retail circulation
↓ | Mall interiors

↑ | **Main view**
↗ | **Interior atrium**
→ | **Different levels,** with escalators

EKZ Rosenberg

Winterthur

This freestanding building appears as a prominent landmark, strategically positioned along the north entrance to Winterthur. The irregular form creates a spatial tension along the various façades, shaping urban public space. The exterior design is structured in two contrasting ways: the public and urban areas at street level, as well as an artificial garden landscape on the plateau level. The residential apartments lead away from the mall level defining the building's silhouette. The scattered concrete voids along the building envelope enhance the unified appearance of the complex. Both entrances to the shopping mall are tied in at street level and made clearly visible with large geometric incisions. The irregular geometry creates three different exteriors.

PROJECT FACTS

Address: Schaffhauserstrasse 152, 8400 Winterthur, Switzerland. **Artists:** Thomas Santhori, Gérard Coquelin. **Client:** Migros Ostschweiz, Anlagestiftung der UBS Personalvorsorge. **Completion:** 2011. **Gross floor area:** 103,000 m². **Additional functions:** residential.

↑ | **Skylights,** from outside
← | **Façade,** entrance

↖ | **First floor plan**
↓ | **Building,** at night

Arup, BDP, Chapman Taylor,
ERA, T+T Design

↑ | **Mall offers 25,000 square meters of retail and leisure space**
→ | **Atrium,** view of retail levels

Forum Istanbul Mall

Istanbul

Forum Istanbul is the biggest shopping mall in Europe. The design offers a contemporary urban experience, interspersed with boulevards, piazzas, avenues, courtyards, and monumental buildings. The interplay of these elements produces streets with sweeping views, narrow lanes, contrasting in scale, and public squares with different spatial qualities. Many components, such as domes, courtyards and oriels were influenced by the local architecture. The colors used reflect the shades of the sea and the hues of spices, with references to Istanbul. A public area with spectacular landscape, it is suitable for venues. Signage, fountains, sculptures and art are also part of the project.

PROJECT FACTS

Address: Barbaros Bulvarı Morbasan Sokak Koza is Merkezi B Blok K 7 Balmumcu, 34349 Besiktas Istanbul, Turkey. **Client:** Multi Turkmall Gayrimenkul Yatırım Insaat ve Ticaret A.S. **Completion:** 2009. **Gross floor area:** 495,000 m². **Additional functions:** aquarium, bowling, cinemas, ice rink, mini golf course.

↑ | **Colors,** reflect shades of the sea and the hues of spices

← | **Sketch of the dome**

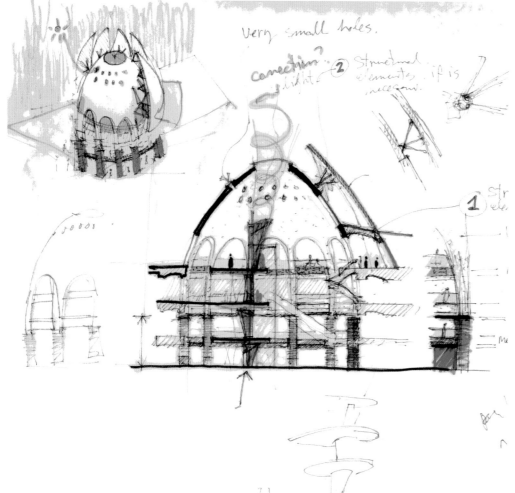

← | **Components,** influenced by local architecture
↓ | **Forum Istanbul,** Europe's biggest mall

HPP Hentrich–Petschnigg & Partner

↑ | **Bird's-eye view**

Rathaus-Galerie

Leverkusen

The design of this new shopping mall is the result of a 2005 investor competition, initiated by the town of Leverkusen. In terms of both urbanization and functionality, the Rathaus-Galerie complex serves as a link between the growing, heterogeneous town and the surrounding structures. This is expressed by the combination of retail and communal functions. With a leasable area of approximately 22,600 square meters and around 5,000 square meters of urban space, this shopping mall presents itself as both open and customer friendly. The round two-story 'Rathaus' sits like a joint on the kinked building base, floating like a UFO above Leverkusen's pedestrian zone.

PROJECT FACTS

Address: Friedrich-Ebert-Platz 2, 51373 Leverkusen, Germany. **Client:** ECE Projektmanagement GmbH & Co. KG. **Completion:** 2010. **Gross floor area:** 74,415 m². **Estimated visitors:** 26,000 per day.

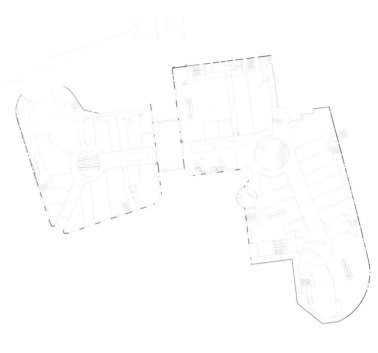

↑ | **Interior design**
↓ | **View from south,** entrance

↑ | **Ground floor plan**

↑ | **Entance**, at night
↗ | **Grassy platform in the central area,**
flower meadow and slope
→ | **Shopping gallery**

La Vache Noire

Arcueil

Located in La Vache Noire, a district built up around a main roadway axis with few green spaces, the program provides an opportunity to create a new hub in the heart of an old urban district. This project places considerable emphasis on its mixed-use function and highlights environmental concerns by transforming the roof over the retail areas into a garden, creating a new public space. The roof folds in on itself, and slopes down to provide access from the adjacent streets. The building is a dynamic ensemble, providing a grassy platform in the central area, a flower meadow, a slope planted with fruit trees and a wood-clad belvedere to the south. The building's main entrance is clearly indicated from the metropolitan intersection by its soaring, pointed roof.

PROJECT FACTS

Address: place de la Vache Noire, RN 20, 94110 Arcueil, France. **Urban planning commercial zone:** François Leclerc. **Landscape architects:** Agence Ter. **Structural engineers:** AVC-Arup. **Client:** Eiffage. **Completion:** 2007. **Gross floor area:** 50,800 m².

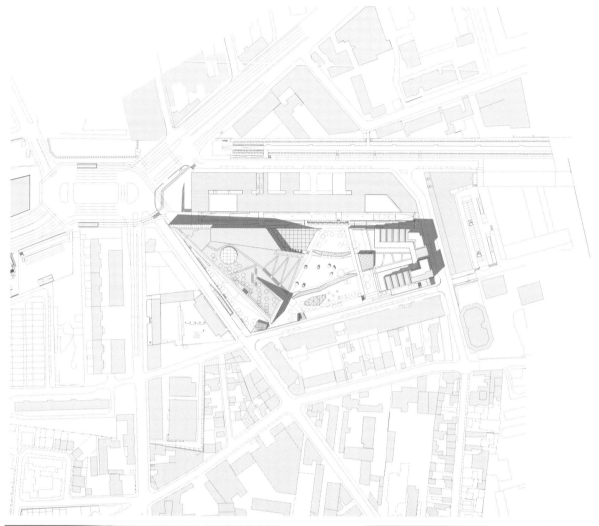

↑ | **Site plan**
← | **Retail area,** detail of the canopy and
circulation

← | Interior view
↓ | Retail area

ATP Architects and
Engineers

↑ | **Main view,** at night
↗ | **Interior,** flooded by daylight
→ | **Entrance**

Varena

Vöcklabruck

This refined construction of pre-tensioned concrete requires very few additional sup-
ports. Featuring filigree ceilings, elegant natural materials and a 'sail' façade that has an
almost hand-crafted appearance, the building is fitted Arcith state-of-the-art energy saving
technology. The location, at the entrance to Salzkammergut in Austria, welcomes a high
number of visitors each year and the design of the forecourt reflects this. The architecture responds to the regional context: "Salzkammergut-summer retreat" 365 days of the
year. The elegant, wide mall forms an endless parade of shopping experiences and houses
80 shops, spread across 32,000 square meters. The sensual interior contours widen out
to form squares and courtyards that invite visitors to relax beneath a friendly, floating
summer-sky.

PROJECT FACTS

225

Address: Linzer Straße 50, 4840 Vöcklabruck, Austria. **Landscape architects:** berchtold land.plan. **Client:** SES Spar European Shopping Centers. **Completion:** 2010. **Gross floor area:** 97,000 m².

↑ | **Multi-story car park**
← | **Gateway**

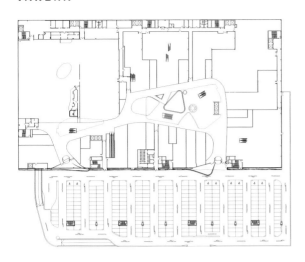

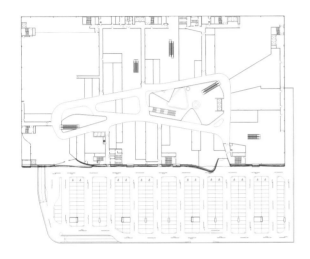

↖ | Ground floor plan
← | First floor plan
↓ | Façade

↑ | Elliptical atrium
↗ | Skylight
→ | Moving walkways towards skylight

Rheinpark Shopping Center

St. Margrethen

After a two-year construction period, the customers of the Rheinpark Shopping Center expect a new shopping experience. Ramseier & Associates from Zurich have completely redesigned this shopping mall with modern colors and materials and the incorporation of a large elliptical atrium that continues from the ground floor all the way up to the roof, allowing an abundance of light into the interior. Clear spatial organization, combined with deliberately chosen color elements and a mixture of natural and artificial light define the mall's new customer-friendly character. The floor of the mall is bright yellow in color, contrasting the elegant anthracite-colored wall cladding and the aluminum ceiling. Orange, black, and white aluminum create a friendly and welcoming atmosphere, which, in combination with the clear spatial organization, offers customers a positive shopping experience.

PROJECT FACTS
Address: Neudorfstraße, 9430 St. Margrethen, Switzerland. **Client:** Genossenschaft Migros Ostschweiz.
Completion: 2009. **Gross floor area:** 26,000 m².

1 Mall
2 Retail area
3 Warehouse
4 Dome skylight
5 Toilets

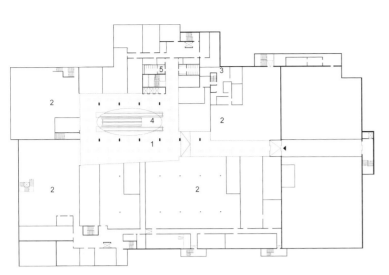

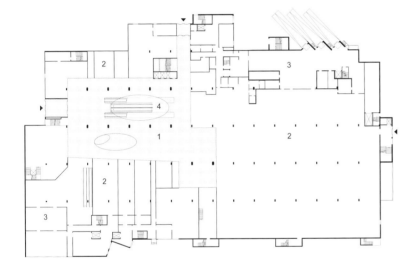

←←| Internal staircase
↖ | First floor plan
← | Ground floor plan
↙ | Basement floor plan
↓ | Section, skylight

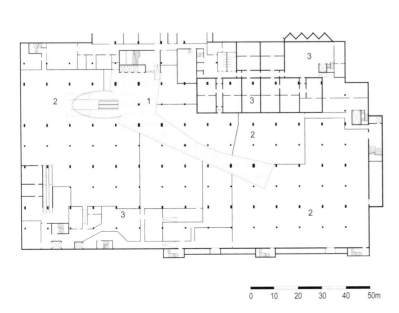

0   10   20   30   40   50m

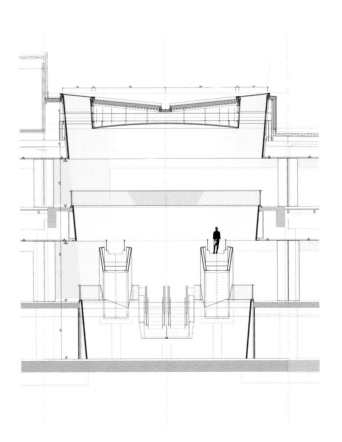

↑ | **Exterior view,** at night
→ | **Interior view**

Liliencarré

Wiesbaden

Liliencarré Wiesbaden is located on the site of Wiesbaden's former main post office, adjacent to the historical main station. At the center of the building ensemble is the oval-shaped, two-story shopping center with approximately 25,000 square meters of retail area, services and restaurants. A domineering brick cube is located along the Adolfsallee, which leads into the city center. As the main volume, this, together with the adjacent row of offices, separates the shopping center from Biebricher Allee and the Carré Terrace from the street.

PROJECT FACTS

Address: Bahnhofsplatz 3, 65189 Wiesbaden, Germany. **Client:** Multi Development Germany GmbH. **Completion:** 2007. **Gross floor area:** 130,000 m².

↑ | **Building ensemble**
← | **Ground floor plan**

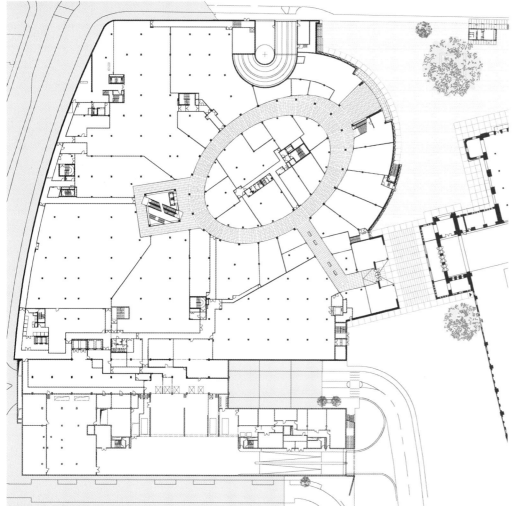

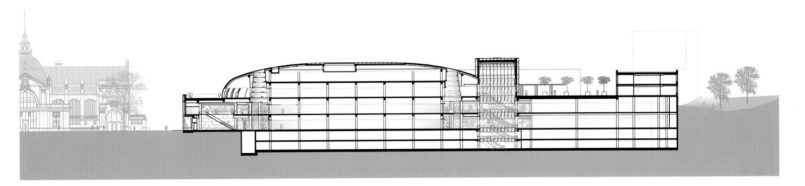

↑ | North elevation and section
↓ | Entrance area

Diener & Diener Architekten

↑ | **Window**, facing west
→ | **Entrance**

Stücki Shopping Center

Basel

The Stücki Shopping Center in Basel was built on the site of a former dye works in close proximity to the French and German borders. Stücki comprises a long hall with four towers, a hotel and a square, facing a street with trees and a small river that feeds into the Rhine. The square and buildings are arranged diagonally to the street. All four towers house the ventilation systems and demarcate the different entrances and exits for pedestrians, lorries and cars. The varied conglomeration of different volumes and façades are unified by the white of the plastered surfaces. Inside, the mall is reminiscent of an archetypical space that has characterized the urban retail trade experience since antiquity: the street and the basilica. Nine domes form four atria on the upper shopping street. These are connected by lifts and ramps to both the ground floor and the parking level below.

PROJECT FACTS

Address: Hochbergerstrasse 70, 4057 Basel, Switzerland. **Landscape architects:** Fahrni und Breitenfeld Landschaftsarchitekten, Vogt Landschafts-architekten. **Lighting designers:** iart interactive. **Client:** Swiss Prime Site AG. **Completion:** 2009. **Gross floor area:** 79,300 m². **Additional functions:** hotel, offices, playland.

↑ | Hotel
← | Interior view

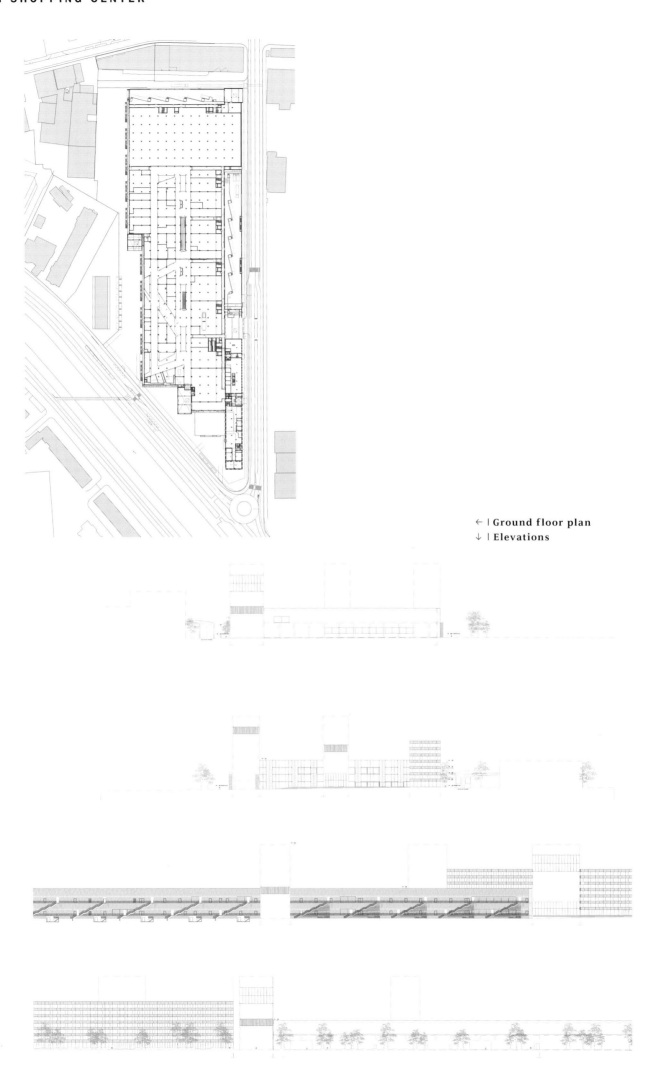

← | Ground floor plan
↓ | Elevations

↑ | **View,** from street
↘ | **Illuminated façade**

↗ | **Interior view**
→ | **Rocket,** surrounded by escalators

Marmara Park

Istanbul

After a construction period of 21 months, the Marmara Park in Istanbul presents approximately 250 specialist stores, restaurants, cafés and a cinema on four floors. The shopping center picks up the "galaxy" design theme. Planet models and illumination create a spectacular outer space atmosphere making the center distinctive. Located in Beylikdüzü-Esenyurt, one of Istanbul's fastest growing districts, the center has a catchment area comprising more than four million people. With 4,000 parking spaces, a nearby metro bus station, several bus lines and its own exit from one of Istanbul's main traffic arteries Marmara Park is excellently accessible.

PROJECT FACTS

Address: Defterdar Yokuşu 3 Tophane, 34425 Karaköy-Istanbul, Turkey. **Completion:** 2012. **Gross floor area:** 100,000 m². **Additional functions:** cinema.

↑ | **Entrance**
← | **Planet models**

← | Entrance
↙ | Ground floor and first floor plans

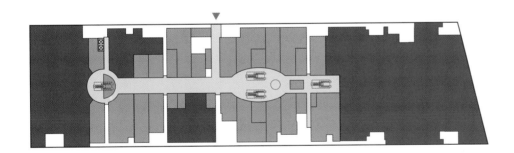

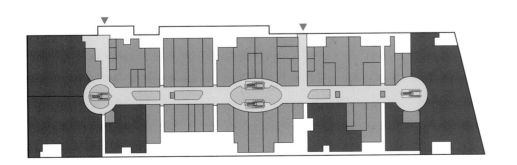

Haskoll (Beijing) Architectural
Design Consultancy

↑ | **Sleek curving lines of the mall finishes**
↗ | **Central void,** four-level chandelier
→ | **External terrace,** dynamic undulating urban
landscape

Euro Plaza

Beijing

The Euro Plaza shopping center is situated to the north east of Beijing City Center, near the
prestigious Eurovillage residential area. Immediately to the north of the site is the newly
completed International Exhibition Center – Euro Plaza is ideally situated to take advan-
tage of both of these developments. Haskoll was responsible for advising on the original
design and retail concept and then improving this where possible. The architects then
developed a new interior design and oversaw the implementation of this on site. The interior of the mall has been designed around the concept of water and earth, where natural
materials have been used in a modern and dynamic way.

PROJECT FACTS

Address: Yu Xiang Road 99, Tianzhu Town, Shunyi District Beijing, China. **Client:** Beijing Oulu Property. **Completion:** 2008. **Gross floor area:** 50,000 m². **Estimated visitors:** 12,000 per day.

↑ | **Strong graphics,** play important role in interior design

↙ | **Main floor plan**

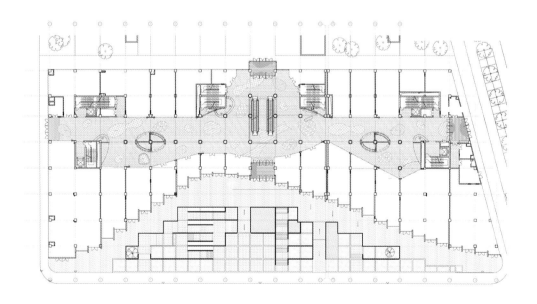

← | **Opening,** clean and simple curved bulkheads
↙↓ | **Sections and detail,** showing central
atrium and chandelier feature

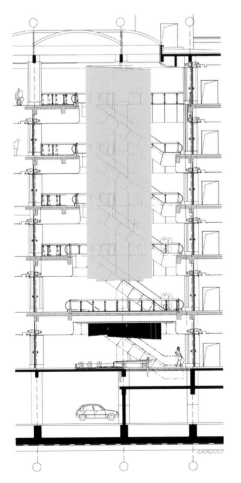

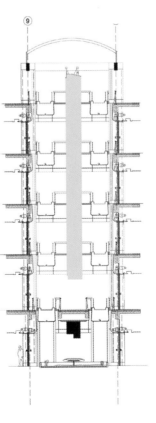

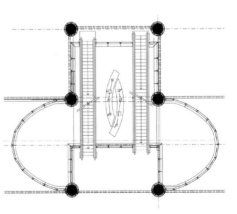

↑ | **Exterior view,** at night
→ | **Façade detail**

Ener[gie]nger

Munich

This showroom and cash and carry for the company Gienger sets a high standard for this industrial park in Munich. The exterior skin comprises solar panels, photovoltaic panels, metal and glass elements. Inviting canopy roofs open out to welcome visitors and create a protected forecourt. Inside, the displays are spread across different levels and connected by ramps, creating an exciting shopping experience.

PROJECT FACTS **Address:** Margot-Kalinke-Straße 9, 80939 Munich, Germany. **Client:** Gienger München KG. **Completion:** 2009. **Gross floor area:** 3,180 m².

↑ | **Building**, in context
↓ | **East elevation**

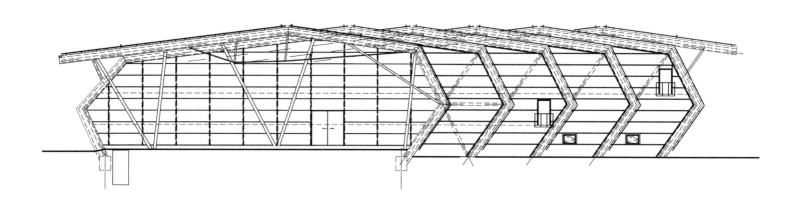

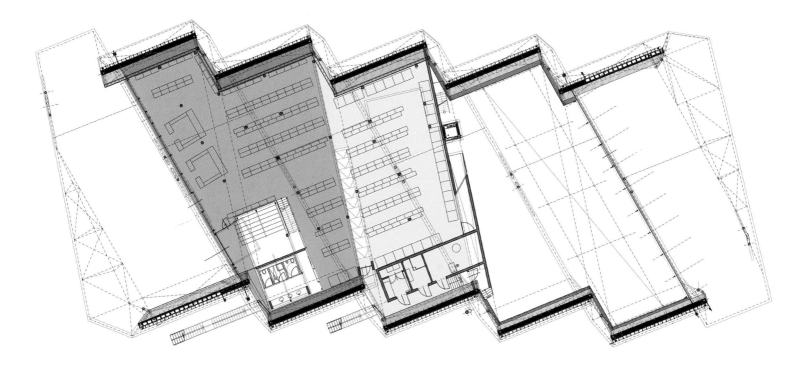

↑ | **Ground floor plan**
↓ | **Façade,** photovoltaic panels

↑ | **Bird's-eye view,** 3D render
↗ | **Mall and external landscape**
→ | **VIP Mall**

Morocco Mall

Casablanca

Morocco Mall, designed by Davide Padoa of Design International, borders the Atlantic Ocean on the Casablanca Corniche coast and is the first and only destination mall in the Mediterranean and Africa. The mall boasts the third biggest musical fountain in the world, a giant aquarium crossed by a panoramic lift, a VIP Mall and the first Galeries Lafayette store in Africa with a Guinness World Record for the the largest in-store façade in the world. The project is characterized by its unique architecture, combining contemporary creative thinking with a bespoke local sensibility, which makes Morocco Mall a new architectural landmark for Casablanca.

PROJECT FACTS

Address: Angle Boulevard de la Corniche, Boulevard de L'Ocean Ain Diab, Casablanca, Morocco.
Landscape architects: DI Landscape. **Client:** Al Amine. **Completion:** 2011. **Gross floor area:**
200,000 m². **Estimated visitors:** 55,000 per day. **Additional functions:** cinema, entertainment and
leisure, semi-public park.

↑ | **Galeries Lafayette store,** with back-lit façade
← | **Aquarium**

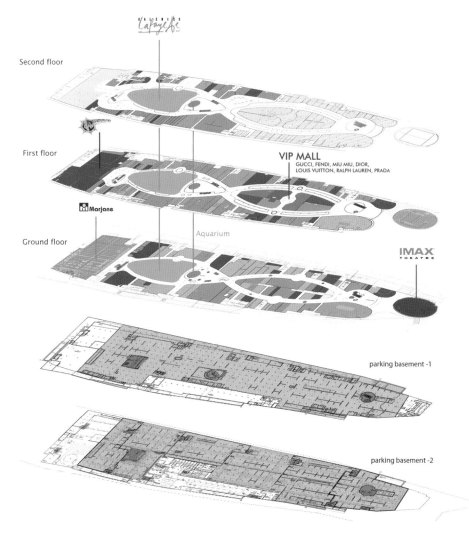

Second floor

First floor

VIP MALL
GUCCI, FENDI, MIU MIU, DIOR,
LOUIS VUITTON, RALPH LAUREN, PRADA

Marjane

Ground floor

Aquarium

IMAX THEATRE

parking basement -1

parking basement -2

← | **Plans,** axonometric
↙ | **Main court,** at night
↓ | **Exterior view,** at night

↑ | **Interior,** main mall
↗ | **Piazza**
→ | **Sawtooth interior**

Médiacité

Liège

The Médiacité project ties together all the disparate elements of its site to create a new axis through the city of Liège. The 350-meter long mall weaves through the fabric of the refurbished old market center at one end, through the new two-story building on the old steelworks site, to connect to the new Belgian national television center at the other. The mall is modeled on the internal 'street' of the traditional galleria and arcade, where the architecture unifies rhythm and proportion. The lattice of steel ribs overhead, mirrored in the floor patterns, sculpts the volume of the mall beneath, drawing a sinuous pathway through each of the zones, revealing diverse vistas and forming a variety of different spatial experiences.

PROJECT FACTS

Address: Boulevard Raymond Poincaré 7, 4020 Liège, Belgium. **Structural engineers:** Buro Happold. **Client:** Wilhelm & Co Group. **Completion:** 2009. **Gross floor area:** 9,750 m². **Additional functions:** recreation center.

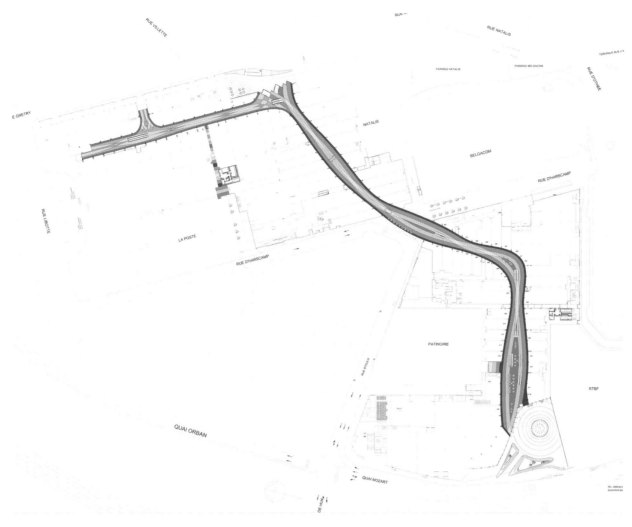

↑ | Ground floor and site plan
← | Construction

↰ | **Piazza terrace**
↓ | **Main view,** across the River Meuse

↑ | **Main view**

El Centre del Món

Perpignan

The New Nuclei Area of the TGV station, which includes the multi-purpose complex with TGV and bus station, mall, offices and two hotels, is the element around which the municipal town planning operation to revitalize Saint Assiscle revolves and makes the new station an intermodal center of urban development and the new economic driving force of the city. The project's two lines of buildings follow an axis parallel to the tracks and create a public street between them. The 400-meter rain screen façade is made of different colored glass, ranging from dark red to deep blue, which gives to the building a dynamic and changing appearance.

PROJECT FACTS

Address: Boulevard Saint Assiscle, 66000 Perpignan, France. **Client:** Metrovacesa Mediterranee. **Completion:** 2011. **Gross floor area:** 71,145 m². **Additional functions:** hotel, offices, railway and bus station, sport facilities.

↑ | **Longitudinal axis view**
↘ | **Section**

↑ | **Pedestrian access,** from Saint Assiscle
↓↓ | **Elevation**

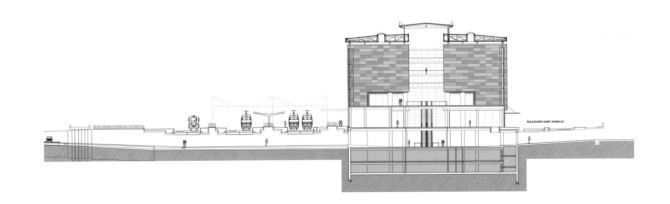

ATP Architects and
Engineers

↑ | **Bird's-eye view**
→ | **Coastline view**

ZTC

Rijeka

ZTC Rijeka, nicknamed "Shopping Center in ate West", is exposed on a hill above the harbor of Rijeka. The three-story building offers spectacular views towards the sea. The distinctive shape of the golden metallic body on a grey concrete base can be seen from far away and stylises the karst landscape behind. The concept of a largely closed building envelope was chosen to reduce solar gain within the building in this exposed location. This ensures efficient cooling of three shopping floors with 20,000 square meters, while the skylights and panoramic glazing offer visitors special amenity value. The design identifies with the city and its contemporary history, and makes a theme of the wider scenery.

PROJECT FACTS **Address:** Janeza Trdine 2, Rijeka, Croatia. **Client:** Universale International, ZTC. **Completion:** 2012. **Gross floor area:** 59,800 m².

↑ | Interior design
← | Urban integration

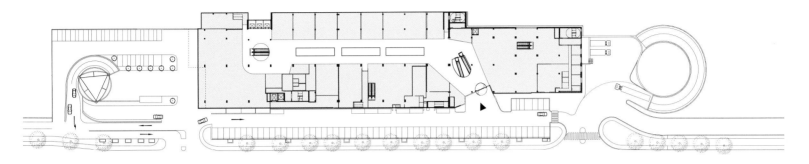

↑ | Ground floor plan
↓ | Façade

↑ | Ground floor plan
↓ | Façade

GAD - Global Architectural
Development

↑ | **Interior view**
↗ | **Interior space,** column-free
→ | **Main view,** seashell-like form

Beşiktaş Fish Market

Istanbul

GAD and Gokhan Avcioglu started the design process with a series of manipulations of the triangular site and its ground surface. To achieve a public and welcoming appearance, the surface was pierced along its periphery. This technique created a hollow, porous form allowing program and circulation to easily mix and flow. The project was developed to form a simple yet iconic concrete and steel seashell-like form covering the entire site with large openings at street level. The sturdy porous shell provides a column-free interior space, optimizing the project's programmatic needs, while also providing a dramatic market space.

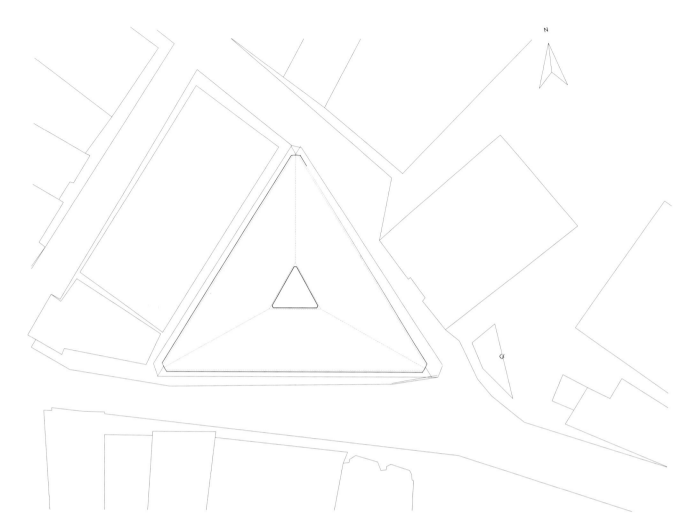

↑ | Site plan
← | Bird's-eye view

← | **Lighting system,** use of hanging light bulbs
↓ | **Section**

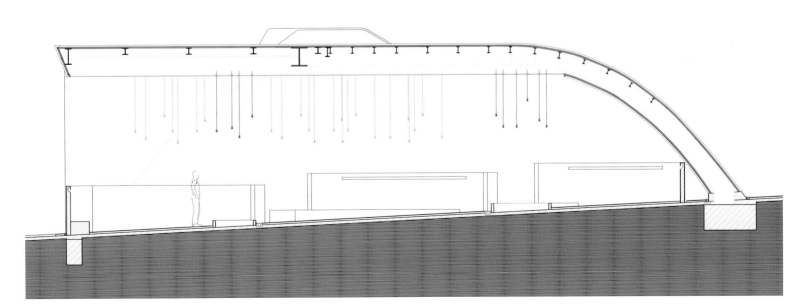

BEŞIKTAŞ FISH MARKET

↑ | **Public square,** with cultural building and shopping center
→ | **Interior development,** void with different levels and green patterns

Forum Mittelrhein

Koblenz

The horizontal structuring of this building has been effectively reduced to accommodate a more human scale. Entrances are positioned at relevant points and invite visitors to "flow" through the building. The trapeze-shaped mall is characterized by soft contours. The atria inside form orientation points, structure the space, and provide plenty of daylight, creating a comfortable atmosphere on the retail level. 740 parking spaces are positioned around a landscaped inner courtyard. The façade design corresponds with the building's function. The two lower floors have a vertically structured glass façade. The upper levels are characterized by the 'vine-covered' façade. This cladding was created with 2,900 identical, three-dimensional aluminum elements, lacquered in three different green shades.

PROJECT FACTS

Address: Zentralplatz, 56068 Koblenz, Germany. **Client:** ECE Projektmanagement GmbH & Co. KG.
Completion: 2012. **Gross floor area:** 67,500 m². **Estimated visitors:** 26,000 per day. **Additional functions:** central square, cultural building.

↑ | Interior design
↙ | Ground floor and site plan

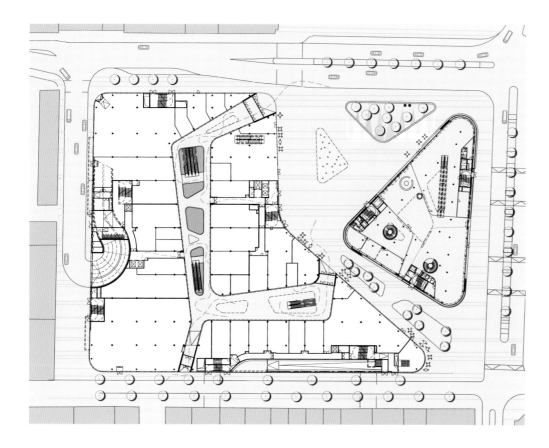

← | **Voids**
↓ | **Exterior façade**, glass and greenery

↑ | **Main view,** entrance by night
↗ | **Shopping gallery**
→ | **Circulation,** escalator

Debenhams Store

Liverpool

The Debenhams project is an integral part of Paradise Street, a major high street in the heart of Liverpool's docklands. Debenhams stands out in the midst of Paradise Street's ubiquitous brick buildings, hitherto the material of choice, which set the tone for the street's somewhat uniform architectural design. Revealing its strategic position and standing out as the district's major point of interest, Debenhams boasts an iconic wave-shaped façade, its curves and counter curves highlighted through an alternation of opaque, translucent and transparent glass.

PROJECT FACTS

Address: Unit 15, 42 Lord Street, Liverpool L2 1TA, United Kingdom. **Client:** Debenhams Grosvenor Estates. **Completion:** 2008. **Gross floor area:** 28,000 m².

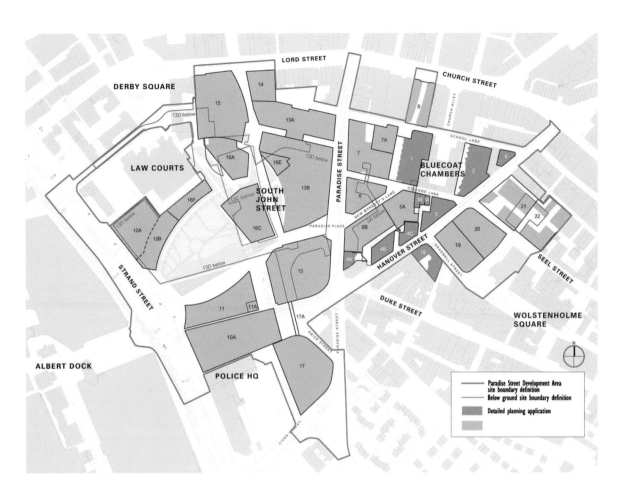

↑ | Master plan
← | Façade detail

← | Entrance
↓ | Main view

Jacobs-Yaniv Architects

↑ | **Wooden beam,** defines upper frame
↓ | **Use of dark materials**
↘ | **Seating area**
↘↘ | **Bar,** along the conservation façade windows

Jaffa Port Market

Jaffa Port

Jaffa Port Market is a new culinary shopping and entertainment venue for food and life-style. The stalls offer a vibrant and exciting experience inspired by the historical, cultural, and culinary legacy of its location at the heart of Warehouse 1, in the regenerated port area on the waterfront. It is open to the port, the docks, and the seafront promenade. The wide area, which formerly functioned as a collection point for goods from all over the world, features a gallery, indoor and outdoor seating areas, and passageways looking into open-plan kitchens that allow visitors to wander amongst the different businesses and experience the huge variety of scents and colors.

Address: Warehouse 1, Jaffa Port, Israel. **Original building:** British mandate, 1930. **Client:** Milgan LTD.
Completion: 2012. **Gross floor area:** 1,200 m². **Estimated visitors:** 1,000 per day.

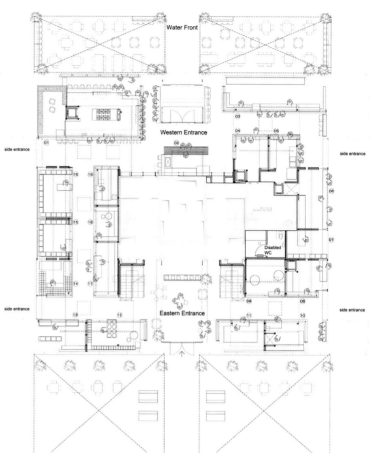

↑ | **Eastern entrance,** seating area
↓ | **Juice bar and decorative wall**

↑ | **Ground floor plan**

RKW Rhode Kellermann
Wawrowsky Architektur +
Städtebau

↑ | **Main view**
→ | **Shopping area**

Milaneo

Stuttgart

The Milaneo in Stuttgart faces the task of giving the sloping site of this former freight yard a new face, integrating it into the existing city center. The new complex will provide space for residential apartments, offices and hotels, as well as shops and restaurants. The three lower levels will house approximately 200 shops, with three additional parking levels located below. The apartments are divided between 17 independent townhouses with individual floor plans.

PROJECT FACTS

Address: Heilbronner Straße, Wolframstraße, Mailänder Platz, 70173 Stuttgart, Germany. **Planning partners:** ECE Architekten. **Client:** ECE, STRABAG Real Estate, Bayerischer Hausbau. **Completion:** 2015. **Gross floor area:** 43,000 m². **Additional functions:** hotel, offices, residential.

↑ | Residential area
← | Bird's-eye view

← | Apartments
↓ | Ground floor plan

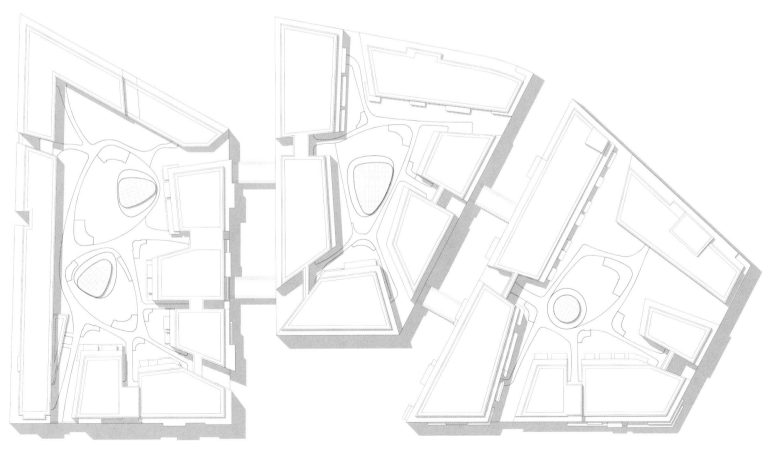

↑ | **Front view**
↗ | **Complex,** comprises six buildings
→ | **Green areas,** open the ensemble

Flagship Designer Outlets

Metzingen

This ensemble comprises transparent and opaque façades – depending on whether the area behind the wall is a display window, entrance, sales room or storeroom. Perforated sections blend with the glass windows and the structures take on a traditional woven pattern. The building envelope indicates Metzingen's earlier importance as a leading location for the textile industry. At the same time, the design documents a love of elegant materials. The two-story entrance areas, which are glazed from floor to ceiling, give the space a generous and welcoming character. The light is filtered through the perforated façade panels, creating a dynamic play of light and shadow inside.

PROJECT FACTS

Address: Reutlinger Straße 69–73, 72555 Metzingen, Germany. **Landscape architects:** Köber Landschaftsarchitektur. **Client:** Holy AG. **Completion:** 2012. **Gross floor area:** 9,369 m². **Estimated visitors:** 11,500 per day.

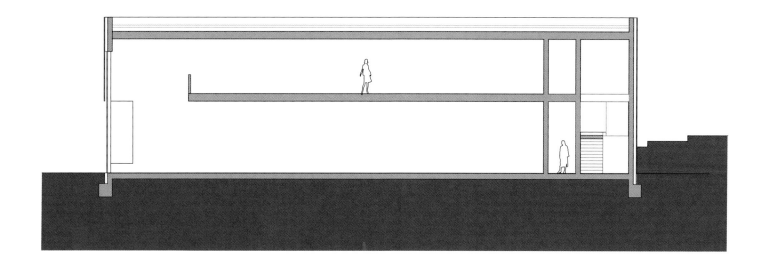

↑ | **Section,** building three
← | **The façades,** resemble textile structures

↑ | **Elegant materials,** combined with natural details

← | **Ground floor plan,** building three

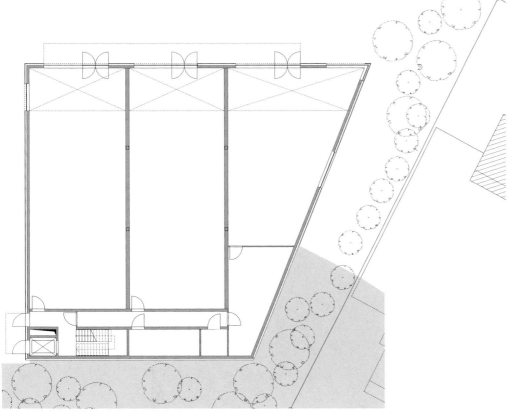

↑ | **Bookshop**
→ | **Street view**

Le Chapeau Rouge

Quimper

The Chapeau Rouge shopping center is located in the heart of a historic neighborhood characterized by narrow plots of land and low-rise granite buildings. The project offers a sensitive and ingenious response to this challenge. It is located on the pedestrian thoroughfare, which provides a much-needed link between the rue de la Providence and the rue du Chapeau Rouge. The shopping center is made up of small shops on a scale, which suits the town and the personality of the newly recreated historic street. The retail center strengthens the character of the neighborhood by re-interpreting its traditional timber frame building methods. The building is resolutely modern with glass and slate shells and metal grilles used as sun protectors, and the corbel arches of its façade offer discreet protection from the weather all along the street.

PROJECT FACTS

Address: rue du Chapeau Rouge, rue de la Providence, rue de Douarnenez, 29000 Quimper, France.
Structural engineers: Cabinet Durand. **Client:** Soderip, Casino Group, Chapeau Rouge SCCV.
Completion: 2011. **Gross floor area:** 5,500 m².

↑ | **Urban integration of the building**
← | **Façade,** pedestrian street

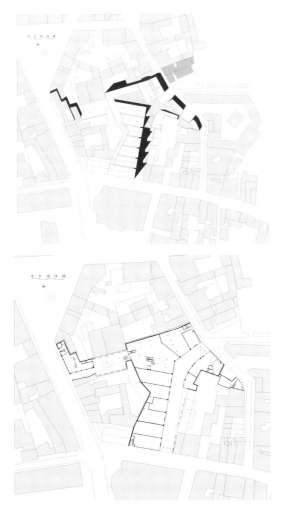

← | **Site plan and ground floor plan**
↓ | **Main view,** by night

↑ | **Exterior wall,** features a unique, large-scale media display
→ | **Each level offers shoppers a different experience**

Hyundai Department Store

Daegu

The goal of this design was to shift perceptions of the Hyundai brand from appealing to a more traditional base to one that taps into a broader demographic. This began with the two exterior façades – a formal, traditional stone base and an overlapping LED animated glass feature wall – creating an icon in the city and expressing the brand's evolution. Inside, the design team created markedly different experiences throughout, providing a unique character for each merchandise district. Beyond the typical retail focused experience, the team also created customer lounges, a cooking school and classroom facilities, a roof-top park, 600-seat auditorium, art gallery and a dining level.

PROJECT FACTS

Address: 200 Kyesan-dong 2-ga, Jung-gu, Daegu, South Korea. **Client:** Hyundai Development Company. **Completion:** 2011. **Gross floor area:** 56,000 m². **Additional functions:** 600-seat auditorium, art gallery, classroom facilities, cooking school, roof-top park.

↑ | **Community-oriented spaces,** encourage people to explore
← | **Store features a new brand identity**

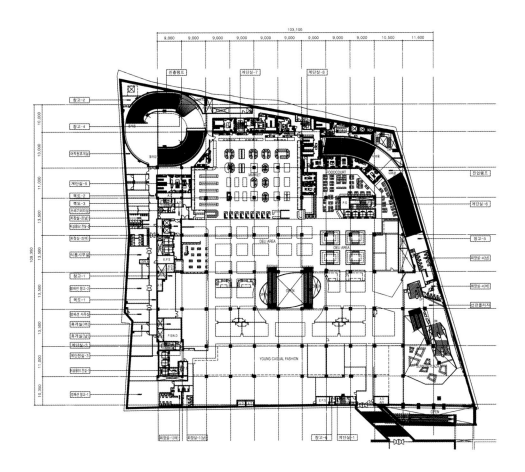

← | **Ground floor plan**
↓ | **Level three,** women's fashion

↑ | **Overall view**
→ | **Atrium,** retail space

Iluma

Singapore

Iluma is an entertainment and retail development located in Singapore's famous Bugis Street area, now a designated arts, education and entertainment quarter. The design contrasts a rectilinear block with a curvaceous sculpted form. The rectilinear element accommodates large, regular components of the car park, retail anchor tenants, cinema and performance spaces, while the curved form accommodates smaller retail and entertainment activities along meandering paths. The dialogue between the two elements is heightened by the architectural treatment, with vibrant hot colors animating the rectilinear block and mono-chrome shades of gray and white cladding the curvilinear block.

PROJECT FACTS

Address: 201 Victoria Street, Singapore 188067, Singapore. **Media façade designers:** Realities United GmbH. **Client:** confidential. **Completion:** 2009. **Gross floor area:** 26,761 m². **Estimated visitors:** 3,000 per day. **Additional functions:** cinema.

↑ | Outdoor plaza
← | Retail levels

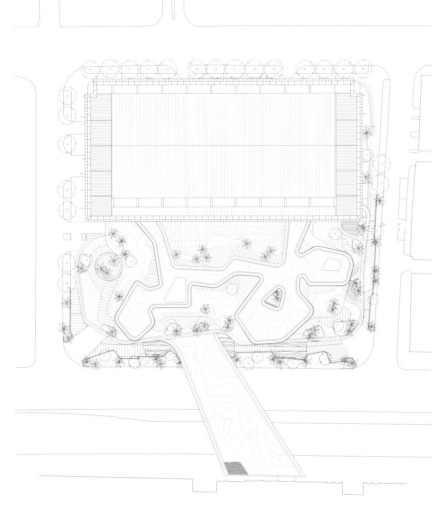

↖ | **Site plan**
↓ | **Façade,** rectilinear block

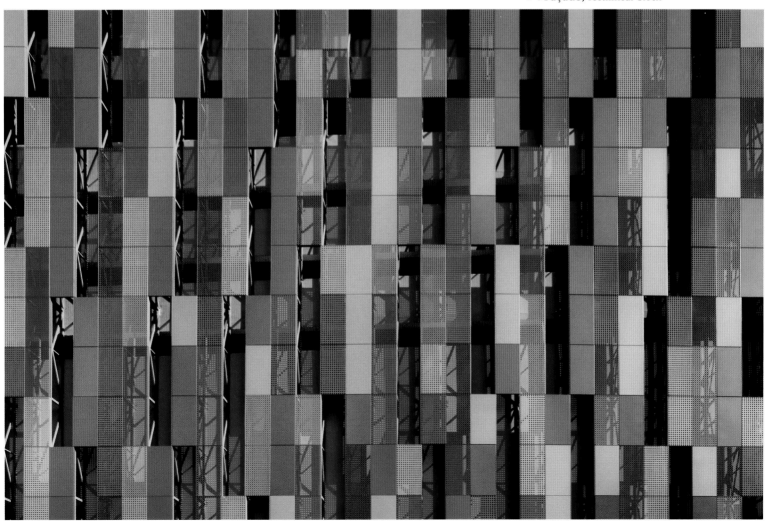

Josep Miàs

↑ | **Main view**, entance
→ | **Interior view**, market stalls

Barceloneta Market

Barcelona

This market seeks to form part of the neighborhood, and is oriented towards both the front and rear of the square. The new metal figures create new market spaces, not touching the ground, but suspended from the old structure, not in a real manner, since the two structures, the old and new, never really overlap structurally, but do so in a false equilibrium. The imprisoned, tamed building writhes within this space, creating a certain violence in the rebuilt form. The building uncurls, curls back up, and offers a succession of new spaces to discover.

PROJECT FACTS

Address: Plaza de la Font 1, 08003 Barcelona, Spain. **Original building:** Antoni Rovira i Trias, 1884. **Structural engineers:** BOMA, Josep Ramón Solé, Maria Ibarz. **Client:** Municipality of Barcelona. **Completion:** 2007. **Gross floor area:** 5,200 m². **Estimated visitors:** 10,000 per day. **Additional functions:** offices.

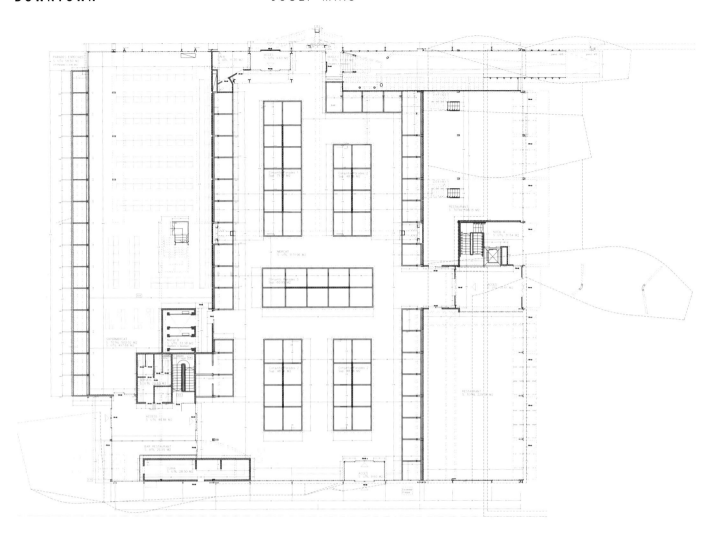

↑ | Ground floor plan
← | Façade detail

← | **Exterior view**, old façade
↓ | **Bird's-eye view**

↑ | **Façade**, tree structure
↗ | **Interior,** display
→ | **Interior**

Zen

Bangkok

Zen is one of the most popular shopping destinations in Thailand, frequented in equal measure by locals and foreigners. During the political riots in Bangkok in 2010, parts of the complex were destroyed by a fire. For the reconstruction, the planners decided on a tree concept as façade structure. It symbolizes not only the environmental consciousness of the design but also the rebirth of the Zen after the fire. The style of the house reflects the wishes and desires of the consumer hungry generation: fun, beauty and cultivated distraction all under one roof.

PROJECT FACTS

Address: World Plaza, 4–4/5 Ratdamri Road, Pathumwan, Bangkok 10330, Thailand. **Original building:** Blocher Blocher Partners, 2007. **Client:** Central Department Store Group. **Completion:** 2012. **Gross floor area:** 93,000 m². **Estimated visitors:** 22,000 per day. **Additional functions:** event hall, offices, sport facilities, training classrooms, wellness.

↑ | Shoe display
↓ | Isometric views

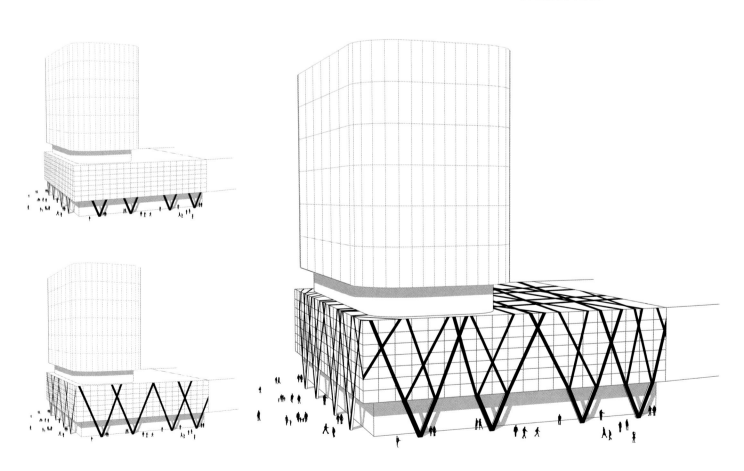

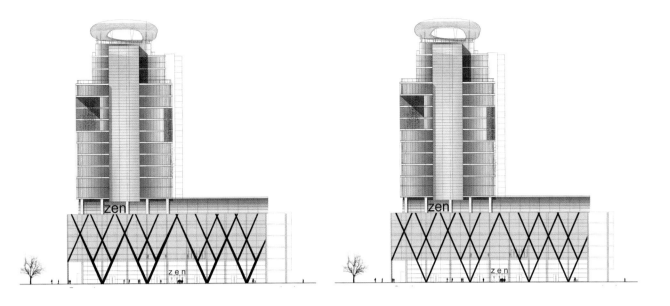

↑ | **Elevations**
↙ | **Exterior façade**
↓ | **Bright and modern store interior**

↑ | **Street view,** spacious historic building from 1885
→ | **Different retail levels**

Shopping Center Grand Bazar

Antwerp

This shopping center is housed in a spacious historic building dating back to 1885 and located on an historic spot in the heart of Antwerp, close to the Groenplaats and the Eiermarkt. The original luxurious and, for the 19th century, innovative design had become faded and was in desperate need of renovation. The design concept by Buro II & Archi+I brings order and homogeneity to the chaotic complex. The uniform and stylish concept focuses on branding and external visibility, architecture and flowing inside circulation. With this project, the building has been returned to its former glory and been given a new character that simply exudes quality.

Address: Beddenstraat 2, 2000 Antwerp, Belgium. **Original building:** Hamaide and E. Van Opstal, 1885. **Client:** Axa Belgium nv Real Estate Division. **Completion:** 2011. **Gross floor area:** 18,500 m². **Estimated visitors:** 17,000 per day. **Additional functions:** hotel.

↑ | **Dynamic shape,** creates flowing spaces
↓ | **Elevation,** exterior façade

← | **White, black and red,** simple and timeless colors
↓ | **Order and homogeneity in the complex chaos**

↑ | Plaza
↗ | Residential area
→ | Public passages stretch underneath the
building

Pillow Terraces

Ljubljana

This complex is located in the heart of Ljubljana, between the park and the main pedestrian street. The program is a mixture of boutique shops, cafés and residences. The street and park are on different levels; a public passage that perforates the building mediates between the two. The lower four floors will house shops connected to a mall, while the top three floors will house apartments. The building is formed in terraces between the low-rise historical line in the park towards the recent extension of the post office on the edge of the plot. Terraces offer views towards the old city and the castle. The lower and largest terrace plateau forms an open air café. An organic mesh wraps the edges of each level, softening the appearance of the building and creating a growth medium for greenery on the façade.

PROJECT FACTS

Address: Čopova ulica, 1000 Ljubljana, Slovenia. **Client:** LE Nepremicnine. **Completion:** 2014. **Gross floor area:** 1,600 m². **Additional functions:** residential.

↑ | **Building**, in context
← | **Undulating façade**

↖ | Main view
↓ | Section

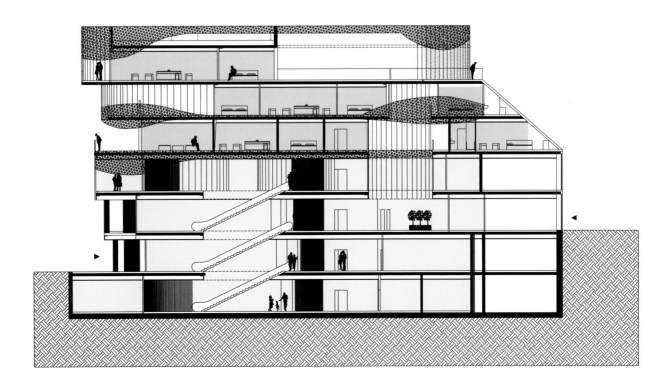

↑ | **Terrace**
↗ | **View to the port**
→ | **Interior view**

Refurbishment of Maremagnum Shopping Center

Barcelona

The objective of the renovation of the second floor of Maremagnum Leisure and Shopping Center was to enable its effective integration into the rest of the center, from which it had been separated. The proposed design benefits from the exceptional location of the center. The design includes a roof garden with belvedere and open terrace surrounded by restaurants with exceptional views of the city, the port and the sea. The new design opens spaces to integrate the complex both visually and functionally.

PROJECT FACTS

Address: Moll d'Espanya 5, 08039 Barcelona, Spain. **Original building:** Albert Viaplana & Helio Piñón, 1993. **Lighting designers:** CA2L. **Client:** Corio. **Completion:** 2012. **Gross floor area:** 7,900 m².

↑ | **Transparent, light-filled design**
← | **Exterior view,** rendering

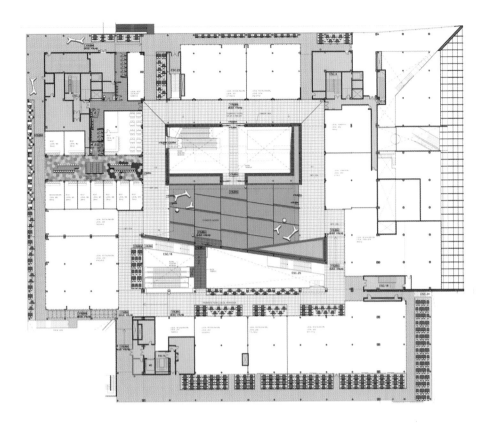

↖ | Ground floor plan
↓ | Shopping gallery

↑ | **Internal atrium,** of CET building
↗ | **Front entrance**
→ | **Entrance,** from plaza

CET

Budapest

The CET (Central European Time) mixed-use development is located at the Közraktár between the Petőfi and the Szabadság Bridge. The CET concept refers to Budapest as an important metropolitan center in the heart of central Europe. The shape of the building is reminiscent of the smooth and streamlined body of a whale. The smooth exterior slides unobtrusively over the edges of the neighboring buildings, adapting to its allotted space. The alternating pattern of the outer shell gives the structure a dynamic appearance. The name and shape of the CET symbolizes its cultural potential and commercial position in one of the world's best preserved cities.

PROJECT FACTS

Address: Fővám tér 11–12, IXth district, 1093 Budapest, Hungary. **Structural engineers:** MTM Statika.
Client: Porto Investment Hungary Kft.. **Completion:** 2011. **Gross floor area:** 27,000 m². **Additional functions:** conference center.

↑ | **Interior,** event space
↓ | **Ground floor plan**

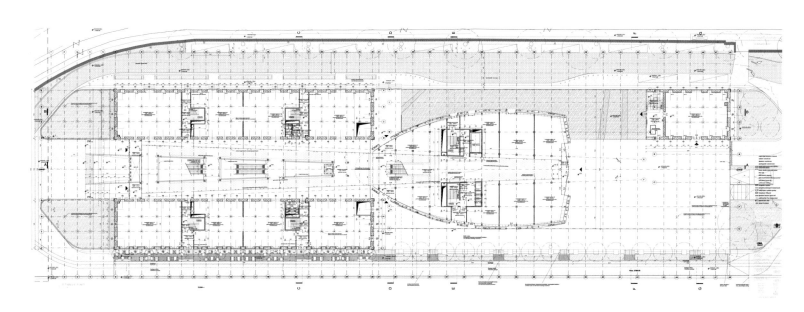

↤ | **Connection,** between old and new buildings
↓ | **Atrium,** escalators between levels

↑ | Hotel entrance
→ | East gallery

Marina Mall

Doha

HOK's designs are inspired by the natural forms created when water and land meet. Five interconnected retail islands, will be enclosed by a simple transparent membrane to create a light, sleek interior. Sculptural pods embedded in the surrounding landscape are designed to animate the public realm between the main complex and the adjacent marina, providing additional retail and leisure facilities. The mall, which totals 60,000 square meters, includes three levels, with an additional 10,000-square-meter hypermarket at basement level. The mall will also house cinemas, restaurants with terraced dining overlooking the marina, and spa facilities.

PROJECT FACTS **Address:** Casamar Compound Building No. 64, Zone 54, Street 639, Doha, Qatar. **Client:** Maz. **Completion:** 2016. **Gross floor area:** 100,000 m². **Estimated visitors:** 35,000 per day. **Additional functions:** cinema, hotel, spa facilities.

↑ | Marina pontoon
← | Section

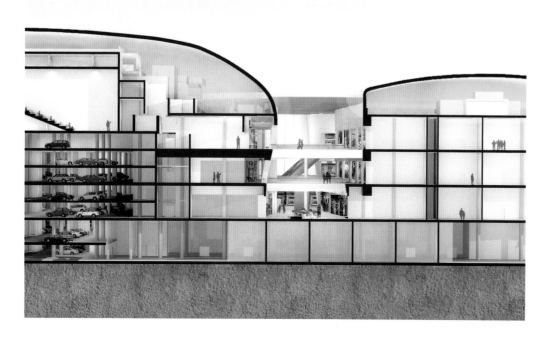

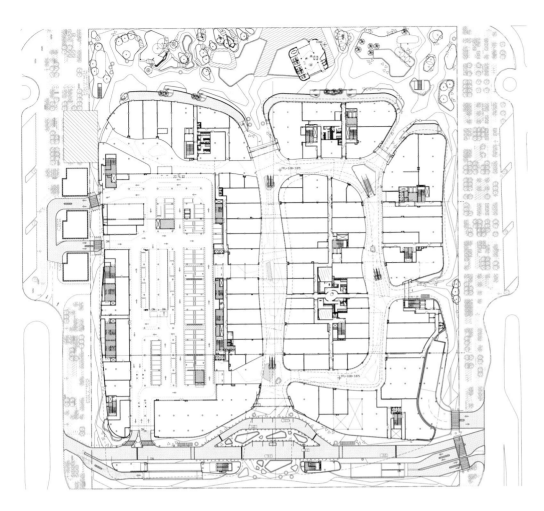

↖ | Ground floor plan
↓ | Bird's-eye view

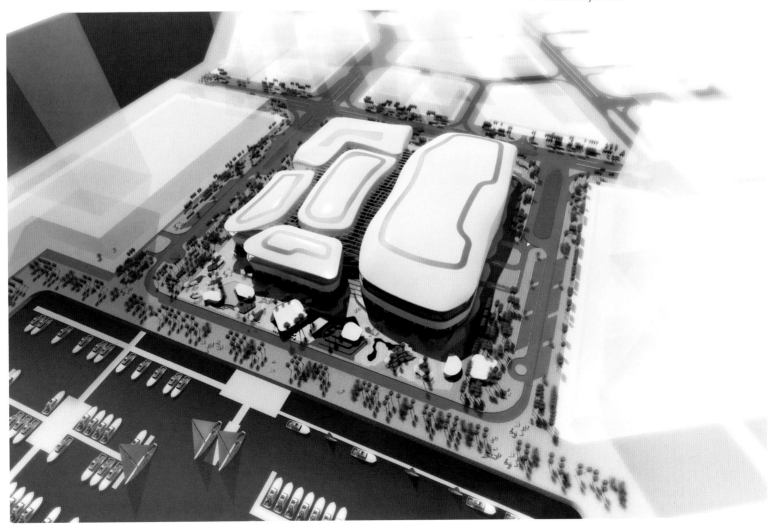

↑ | **Brick façade**
↓ | **Elevation**

→ | **Inner shopping passageway,** with glass roof

Forum Duisburg

Duisburg

Forum Duisburg, together with the Mercator department store, create Duisburg's new city center. This new type of urban shopping center arranges the sequence of shops, alleyways and small squares all under one roof, with the intention of creating the desired inner-city atmosphere. The large glazed entrance opens out towards the Königstraße, a glass-roofed passageway leads past the shops and into the centrally located 'market hall'. All four levels offer a rich variety of shops.

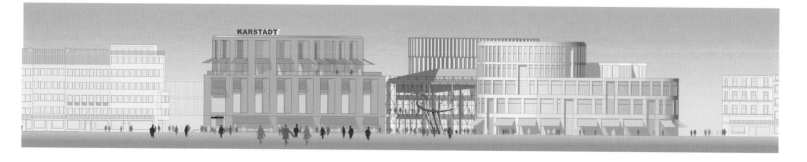

PROJECT FACTS

Address: Königstraße 48, 47051 Duisburg, Germany. **Client:** Multi Development Germany GmbH.
Completion: 2008. **Gross floor area:** 107,000 m².

↑ | **Retail passages,** with glass roof above
↙ | **Ground floor plan**

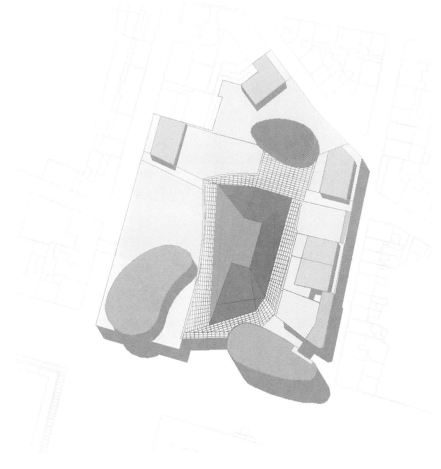

↖ | Site plan
↓ | Street view

B+W architecture Ueli Brauen
+ Doris Wälchli

↑ | **La Miroiterie building,** by night
↓ | **Interior design,** focuses on concrete and glass

→ | **Illuminated façade,** at night

Shopping Mall La Miroiterie

Lausanne

The construction of the La Miroiterie commercial building is closely linked to the Parking du Centre by a common complex structural logic. The three-story construction over a glazed ground-floor hall is raised on top of the car park, which forms its base. It is supported by a tree-like system of branches, which transfers the load to the structural spine of the car park. The balance of this precarious-looking construction is stabilized by the supporting core located at the back of the building. The façades are constructed with translucent, pneumatic cushions. The membranes of these cushions are stretched between the large diagonal wind-bands. Crystalline structures as well as the soft, quilted effect of the textiles are the reference points that determine the extraordinary ambivalent character of the building.

PROJECT FACTS **Address:** 11, Rue du Port-Franc, 1003 Lausanne, Switzerland. **Planning partners:** Hightex International AG. **Client:** Mobimo Management SA. **Completion:** 2007. **Gross floor area:** 2,095 m².

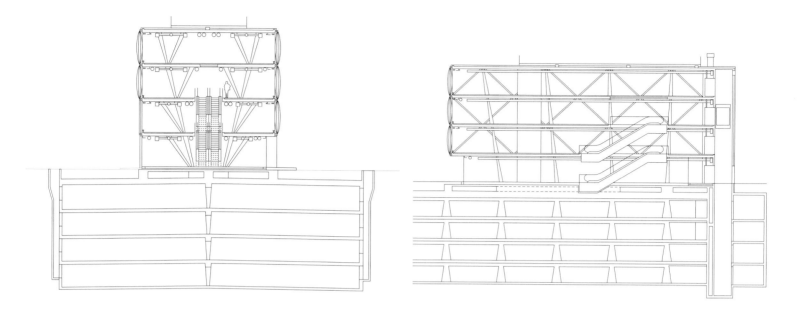

↑ | Longitudinal and cross sections
← | Façade detail

↑ | Illuminated façade
↓ | Layout plans

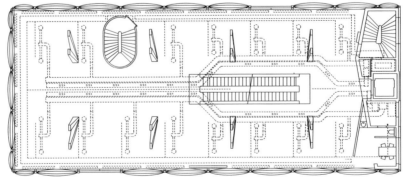

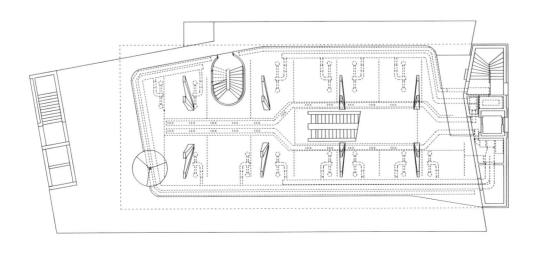

↑ | **Main view,** from Königsplatz
↓ | **Façade detail**
↘ | **Interior view,** atrium
↘↘ | **Façade,** moiré pattern

City Point

Kassel

The volume of the new department store fits the curvature of the Königsplatz. The exterior façade membrane is made of imprinted single-pane white safety glass approximately 43.30 x 1.60 meters. The membrane continues with the same dimensions over the rounded-off building corners. The pattern imprinted in the panes, which was designed by documenta artist Thomas Bayrle, shows pictures of Kassel and enhances the changing incidence of daylight into a dynamic play of shadows on the façade. Individual controllable sources of light generate different moods for evening and night illumination.

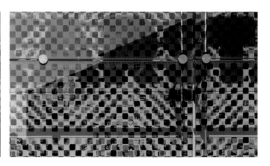

PROJECT FACTS **Address:** Königsplatz 61, 34117 Kassel, Germany. **Artists:** Thomas Bayrle. **Client:** ECE Projektmanagement. **Completion:** 2001. **Gross floor area:** 20,000 m². **Estimated visitors:** 35,000 per day.

↑ | **Arcaded sidewalk**
↓ | **Site plan**

↑ | **Exterior view,** from Königsstraße

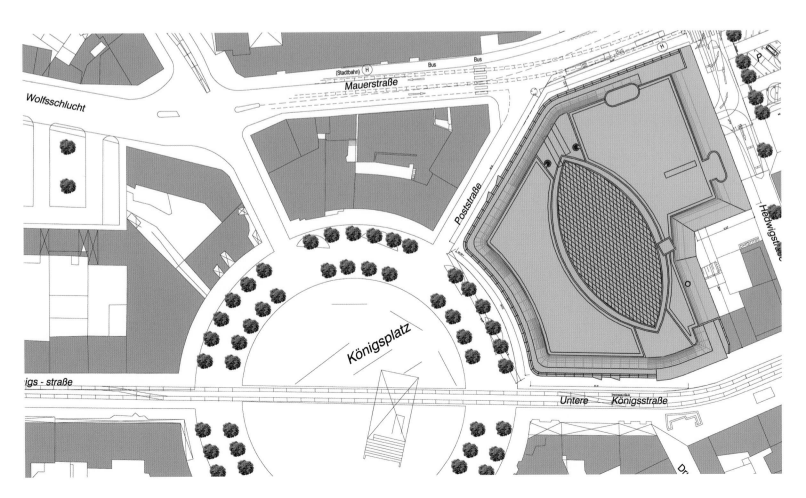

↑ | **Book City,** retains parts of the original building
→ | **Choice of materials,** establishes a dialogue with the surrounding architecture

Book City

Ningbo

The Taifeng Floor Mill creates an industrial silhouette in the center of Ningbo. A focus of the conversion of this historical building to Book City was to retain the architectural insignia, the silo, and the high stair towers. Designed as a 'city within a city', Book City is a mixed-use store housing a mega bookstore, cultural facilities, modern office space and restaurants. The extensions added to the original building have given it a new urban appearance. In the center, the Xinghua Book Store has been built to resemble an open book. The use of brick and crystal-shaped sun protection grids creates a dialogue with the Tianyi Pavilion, the oldest private library in China.

PROJECT FACTS **Address:** 768 Lingqiao Road, 315000 Ningbo, China . **Client:** Ningbo Newspapering Group. **Completion:** 2010. **Gross floor area:** 65,000 m². **Estimated visitors:** 10,000 per day. **Additional functions:** cultural facilities, offices.

↑ | **Book City,** at night
← | **Interior view**

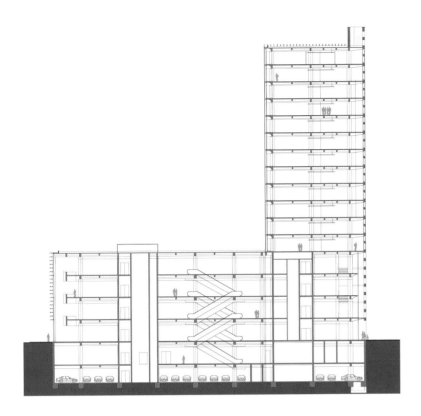

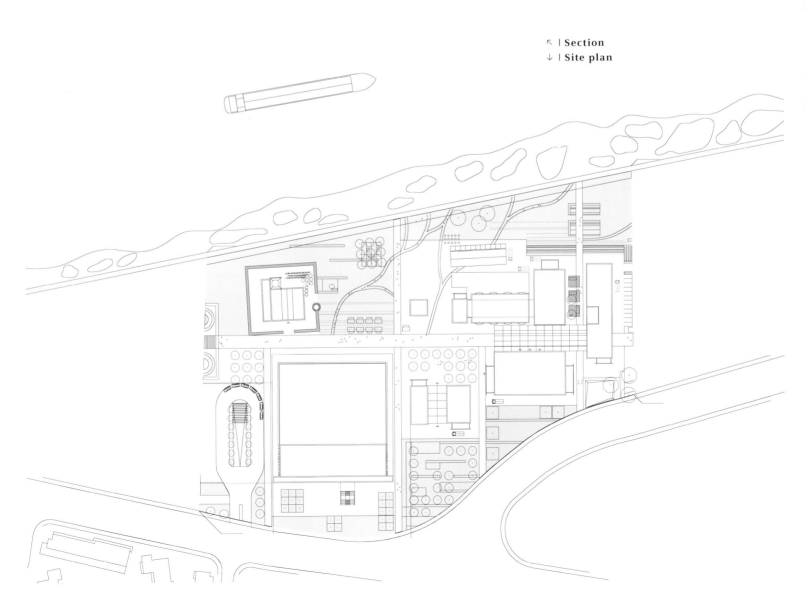

↖ | Section
↓ | Site plan

↑ | **Shop windows as curvaceous frames**
→ | **Illuminated shop windows at night**

Chungha Building

Seoul

MVRDV have transformed the appearance of this mixed-use building into a modern glowing beacon for the Gangnam area. The original concrete building was built in the 1980s and houses a leather accessories store on the ground floor. The upper floors accommodate private businesses. The new windows have been made as large as possible and are used by tenants for display purposes. The outer surfaces of the window boxes have curved edges and the surfaces are clad with tiny mosaic tiles.

PROJECT FACTS **Address:** 100-33 Cheongdam-dong, Gangnam-gu, Seoul, South Korea. **Original building:** 1980s. **Lighting designers:** Total LED. **Client:** Woon Nam Management Co. Ltd.. **Completion:** 2013. **Gross floor area:** 2,820 m². **Additional functions:** offices.

↑ | **View from the street**
← | **Elevation**

← | **Façade detail**, mosaic tiles following the curvature
↓ | **Section**

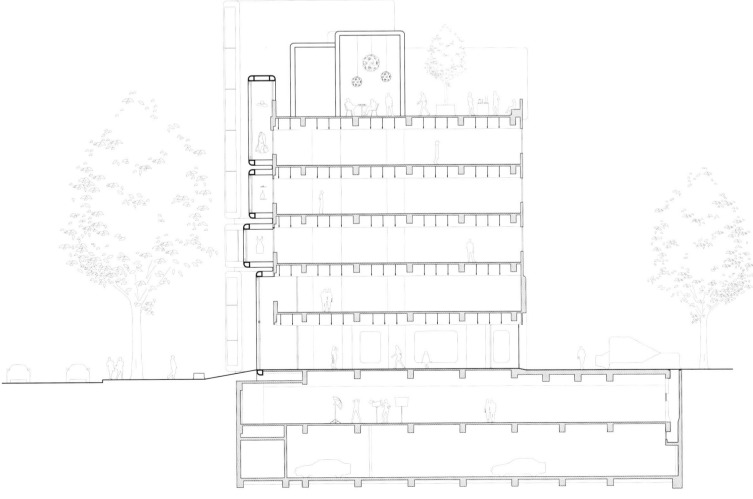

↑ | **Center court grand plaza,** retail terraces
↗ | **Bloomingdales,** entry at night
→ | **City side-entry**

Santa Monica Place

Santa Monica

Commissioned to renovate an outdated 1980s-era mall, Jerde set out to create a vibrant public setting and real urban space rather than a shopping center. Blending timeless urban principles that predate conventional malls with its organic approach to retail design, Jerde carefully and intricately weaved the project into the existing city fabric. The design opened up the mall by removing the roof, creating generous open spaces, and establishing pedestrian connections that extend the famous Third Street Promenade and strengthen the surrounding city core. By incorporating forms, materials, and landscaping that are found throughout the city, Jerde enhanced the project's natural fit, both aesthetically and funtionally, in the coastal city.

PROJECT FACTS

Address: 395 Santa Monica Place, Santa Monica, CA 90404, USA. **Original building:** Frank Gehry, 1980.
Landscape architects: LRM. **Lighting designers:** Kaplan, Gehring, McCarroll Lighting Design. **Client:**
Macerich. **Completion:** 2010. **Gross floor area:** 50,000 m².

↑ | **Third Street promenade,** day view
← | **Center court plaza,** in the evening

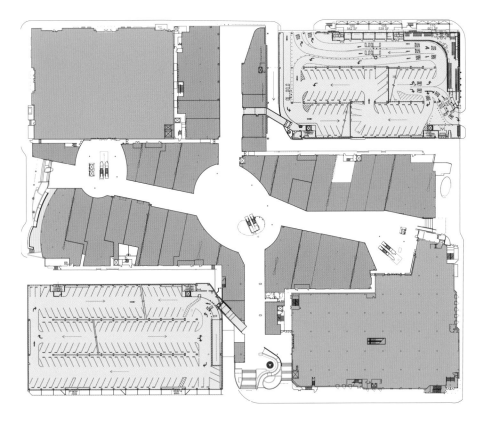

↖ | **Ground floor plan**
↓ | **Third Street promenade,** seamless connection

Lifschutz Davidson
Sandilands

↑ | **Fruit and honey store**
→ | **Restaurant**

Tsvetnoy Central Market

Moscow

This project involved a 4,666-square-meter fit-out in a new department store on Moscow's Tsvetnoy Boulevard. The new store offers three floors of food, retail and restaurant space, with a spectacular destination rooftop café, in the six-story retail concept on the site of Moscow's historic Central Market. A spectacular ceiling of beaten stainless steel relates directly to the geometry of the external envelope and wraps around the levels. The highly polished steel reflects the wares and visitors below with constantly shifting patterns reflecting light from the deep windows over Tsvetnoy Boulevard and the skylight on the top floor.

PROJECT FACTS
Address: Tsvetnoy Boulevard, Moscow 127051, Russia. **Client:** RGI International. **Completion:** 2011.
Gross floor area: 4,666 m².

↑ | **Main atrium escalators**
← | **Interior view**

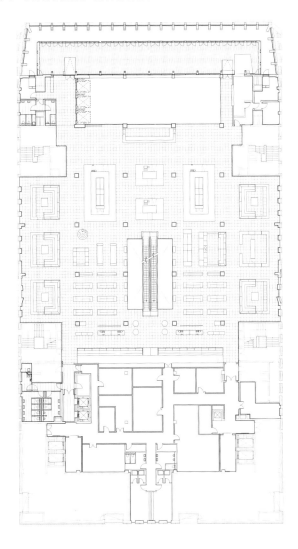

← | **Fifth floor plan,** market area
↓ | **Section,** central atrium

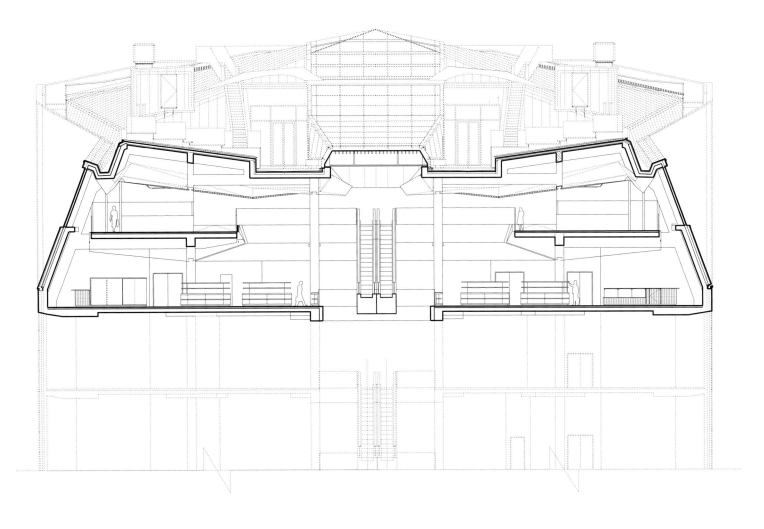

↑ | **Buildings form a family,** with smooth façades designed to need little maintenance
→ | **Façade pattern,** developed with a scholar of Islamic arts

Aldar Central Market

Abu Dhabi

Abu Dhabi's Central Market is one of the oldest sites in the city. Open at night as well as during the day, these new spaces provide an important central venue in the city during festivals and celebrations. The spaces can be enclosed by roof panels that slide into place to enable the internal environment to be controlled more easily. The site is generously landscaped, with the roofs of the podium buildings forming a series of terraced gardens. By offering an alternative to the globalized one-size-fits-all shopping mall this building offers a distinctive modern interpretation of the regional vernacular.

PROJECT FACTS

Address: Hamdan Bin Mohammed Street, Abu Dhabi, United Arab Emirates. **Structural engineers:** Halvorson & Partners. **Client:** Aldar Properties. **Completion:** 2014. **Gross floor area:** 607,000 m². **Estimated visitors:** 20,000 per day. **Additional functions:** cinema, office, residential, two hotels.

↑ | **Dappled sunlight, bright colors and fountains,** changing rhythm of squares, court-yards and alley ways
← | **Shopping street**

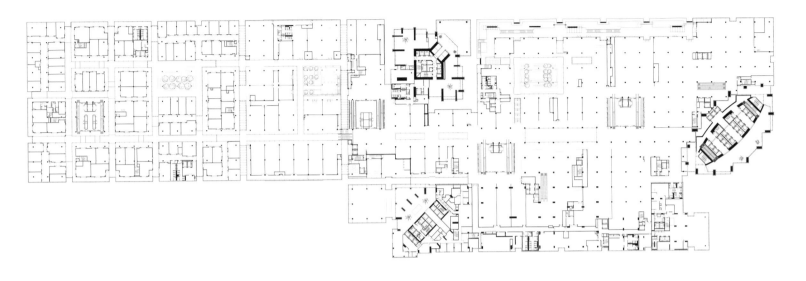

↑ | **Ground floor plan**
↓ | **Courtyard,** with cafés and restaurants

↑ | Exterior at dusk
→ | Rooftop terrace

D-Cube City

Seoul

Located in the dense capital city of Seoul, South Korea, and connected to the city's busiest metro line, D-Cube City represents a significant new model for urban land use related to intelligent mixed-use, transit-oriented development. The new cultural and commercial destination is one of the city's first fully integrated developments, made up of a six-level retail, entertainment and culture complex with a major performance hall as its rooftop centerpiece, a 42-story landmark office and hotel tower, and over six acres of new public landscape, parks and plazas. Two adjacent 50-story residential towers complete the new urban complex.

PROJECT FACTS

Address: 692 Shindorim-Dong Guro-gu, Seoul, 152-888 South Korea. **Executive architects and residential tower designers:** SAMOO Architects&Engineers. **Landscape architects:** Oikos Design. **Lighting designers:** LPA, Newlite. **Water features:** Fluidity. **Client:** Daesung Industrial Co. Ltd. **Completion:** 2011. **Gross floor area:** 320,000 m². **Estimated visitors:** 80,000 per day. **Additional functions:** entertainment, hotel, office, residential.

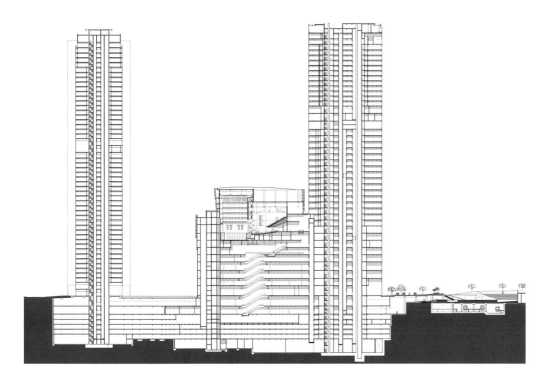

←←| **Main interior,** retail volume
↖ | **Section**
← | **Outdoor public space,** below culture venue

Ibelings van Tilburg
Architecten

↑ | Communal garden
→ | Mall and residential building

De Karel Doorman

Rotterdam

The Karel Doorman project comprises the renovation of a shopping building and the addition of a residential building. The new residential building is up to 70 meters in height and houses 114 apartments. It is built on top of the Ter Meulen Tbuilding in Rotterdam. The Ter Meulen building was constructed in 1948 as a shopping center for Ter Meulen, Wassen and Van Vorst and designed by Van den Broek and Bakema. Ibelings van Tilburg architecten proposed not to demolish the building, but to restore the Ter Meulen building to its original condition. Both of the floors from 1977 have been demolished to make place for the new apartment building. While the Ter Meulen building itself has been restored to its original condition, the design for the new addition is abstract. The new apartment building features a glazed, printed external skin.

PROJECT FACTS

Address: Karel Doormanstraat 386J, 3012 GR Rotterdam, The Netherlands. **Original building:** van den Broek en Bakema, 1948. **Client:** DW Nieuwbouw. **Completion:** 2012. **Gross floor area:** 22,950 m². **Additional functions:** communal garden, residential.

↑ | **Front view**
↓ | **Ground floor plan**

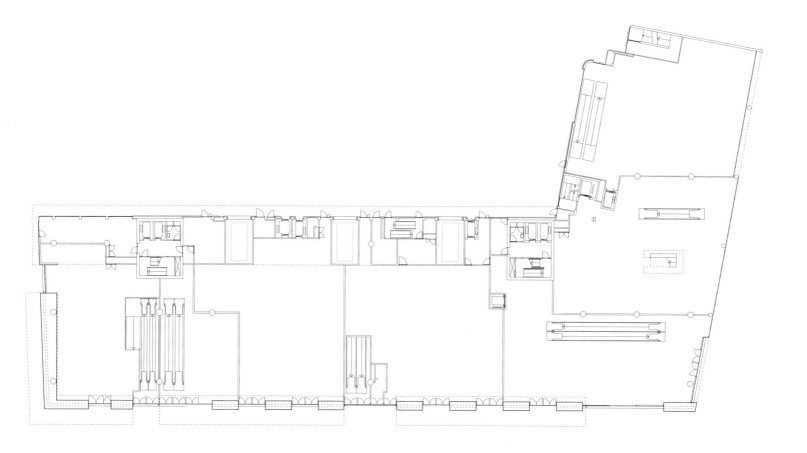

↑ | Condition of the Ter Meulen building in 2001
↖ | Bird's-eye view
↓ | Front elevation and section

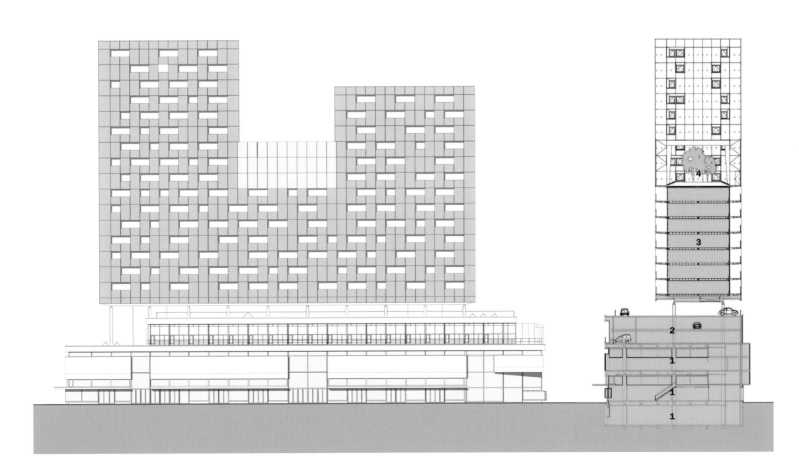

Manuelle Gautrand
Architecture

↑ | **South entrance**
↓ | **Elevation**

↗ | **South-west entrance**
→ | **Interior view**

Galeries Lafayette

Annecy

Designed in the 1970s, the building of Galeries Lafayette Shopping Mall in Annecy was built completely independently, without any background research on context, form, alignment, or density. The goal of this new extension was both to preserve the building's now historic qualities and at the same time rejuvenate it with an innovative and bold architecture. The objective of the project was to modernize the existing surfaces and create a large extension to house numerous retail stores in addition to the Galeries Lafayette existing premises. The project consists of several circular volumes that slide above and below the existing volumes. These are five satellites that cluster around the existing volumes and along the west and south façades, forming a sort of constellation of circular volumes. At the center of the project is a large square that is bathed in natural light through the glass roof above.

PROJECT FACTS

Address: 25, avenue du Parmelan, 74000 Annecy, France. **Original building:** 1970. **Client:** Citynove - Groupe Galeries Lafayette. **Completion:** 2015. **Gross floor area:** 9,000 m².

↑ | **Night view,** colorful lighting
↓ | **Concept scheme**

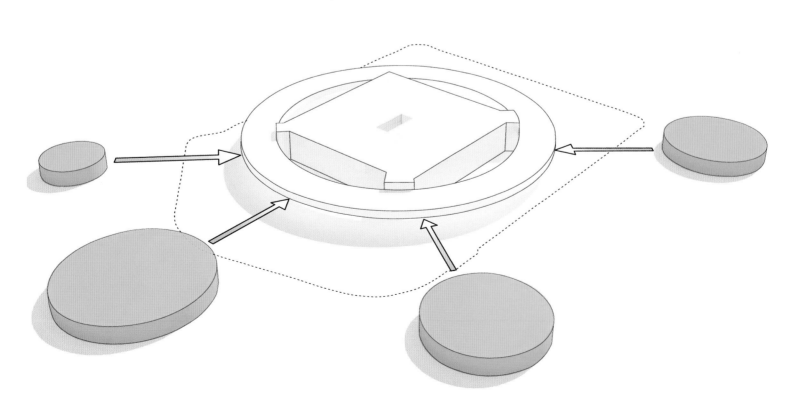

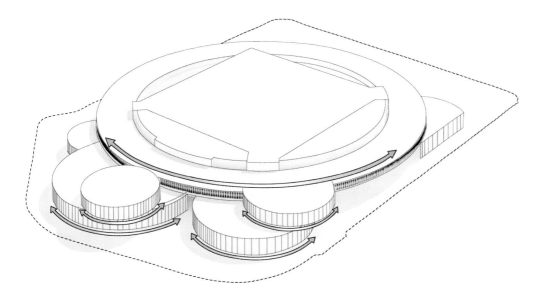

↖ | Concept scheme
↓ | West entrance

↑ | **Front view**
↗ | **Old trees,** have been kept
→ | **Interior view**

Daikanyama Tsutaya Books

Tokyo

Located in an up-market but relaxed shopping district, KDa's new Daikanyama T-Site is a collection of buildings for Tsutaya, a giant in Japan's book, music, and movie retail market. Drawing on all KDa's design skills – architecture, interior, furniture and product display – the project's ambition is to define a new vision for the future of retailing. Slotted between large existing trees on the site, the three pavilions are organized by a 'magazine street' that threads through the complex, blurring interior and exterior. Tailored particularly to over-50 customers, Tsutaya's normal product range is complimented by a series of boutique spaces carrying carefully curated product ranges. Other facilities include a café, an upscale convenience store, and the Anjin lounge, where visitors can browse a library of classic design magazines and books or peruse artworks for sale as they eat, drink, read, chat, or relax.

PROJECT FACTS

Address: Sarugaku-chou, Shibuya-ku, Tokyo. **Interior designers:** Bauhaus Maruei, D. Brain, Hand Factory. **Landscape architects:** Furuuchi Sekkeishitsu. **Client:** Culture Convenience Club. **Completion:** 2011. **Gross floor area:** 5,607 m². **Additional functions:** residential.

↑ | **Three buildings,** connected by bridges of polished stainless steel
← | **Entrance,** façade reflects the Ts of the Tsutaya logo

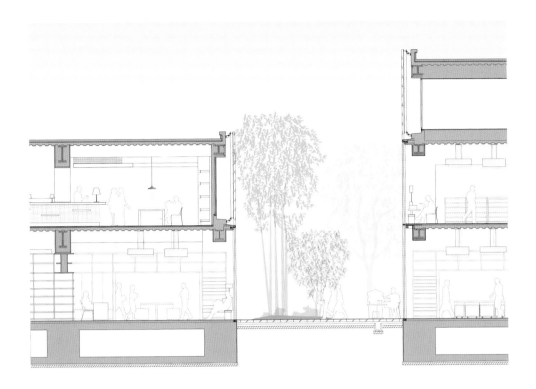

↖ | Section
↓ | Ground floor plan

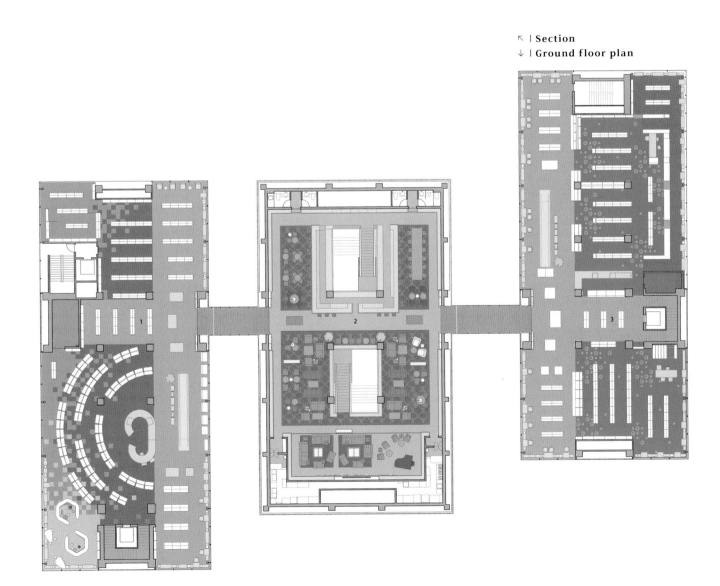

3deluxe

↑ | **Façade**
→ | **Varying designs,** create intriguing
layered effects and a visual impression of depth

Zeilgalerie

Frankfurt/Main

The redesign of the Zeilgalerie shopping center, which opened in 1992 and is renowned far beyond Frankfurt's city limits, includes a completely new look for the façade and a makeover of the public areas inside the complex. As it is the only exterior view of the complex enclosed on three sides, the façade facing out onto the Zeil shopping mall is representative of the entire architecture – the perception of shape gets reduced to the perception of space. The façade's unusual black and white colors, its filigree ornamentation and the integrative interaction of architecture, graphic design and light orchestration create a distinctive character for the building on Zeil.

PROJECT FACTS

Address: Zeil 112, 60313 Frankfurt/Main, Germany. **Original building:** Kramm & Strigl, 1992. **Media installation:** Meso Digital Interiors. **Client:** IFM Immobilien AG. **Completion:** 2011. **Gross floor area:** 14,700 m². **Estimated visitors:** 15,000 per day. **Additional functions:** cinema, roof terrace.

↑ | **19,700 light diodes,** create a large variety of aesthetic light images
← | **Entrance**

← | Contrasting interior design
↓ | Elevation

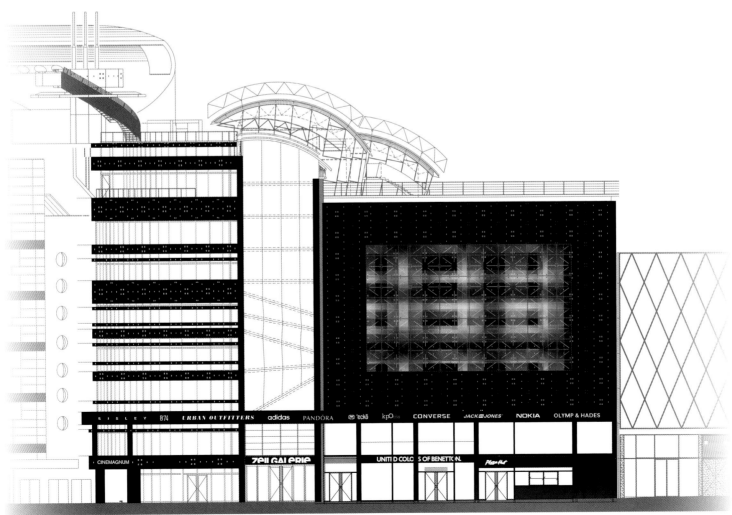

↑ | **View from ground**
→ | **Façade**

Kö-Bogen

Düsseldorf

Kö-Bogen, currently under construction, is a six-story office and retail complex in downtown Düsseldorf and marks an important transition between urban space and landscape. Two city blocks will be joined with one continuous roof line, forming a unified space for walking, shopping and working. The building will also create a connected space between the Schadowplatz, a pedestrian street, and the Hofgarten, the central park in Düsseldorf. Permeated cuts into Kö-Bogen itself will allow for the landscape to naturally blend and flow into the building space. The green courtyards and green roof become part of a new environment that bridges urban space with park space, a fitting entrance to and from the Hofgarten.

PROJECT FACTS

Address: Schadowstraße 12, 40212 Düsseldorf, Germany. **Façade designers:** Murphy Facade Studio + Infacon. **Client:** die developer. **Completion:** 2014. **Gross floor area:** 40,165 m². **Additional functions:** green courtyards, offices, two-story connecting bridge with roof terrace.

↑ | **Construction**
← | **Kö-Bogen,** forms a connection to the Hofgarten

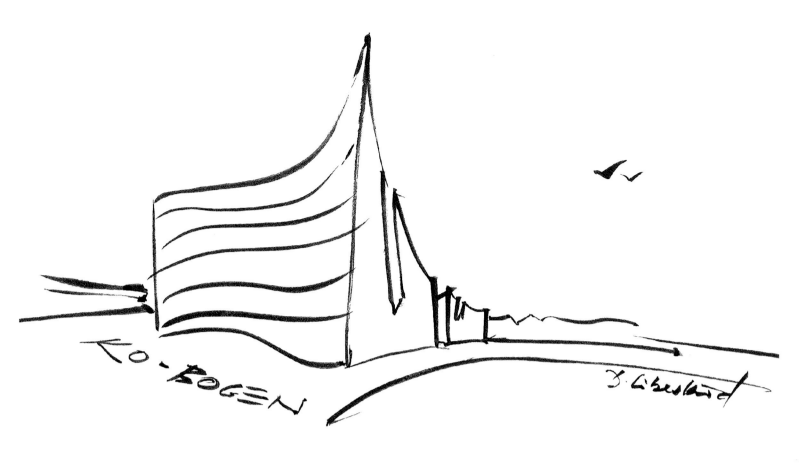

↖ | Sketch
↓ | Courtyard entrance

John McAslan + Partners

↑ | **Retail levels**
→ | **Skylight above,** allows light to flood into atrium

Peter Jones

London

John McAslan + Partners completed the phased refurbishment of the John Lewis Partnership's flagship department store, Peter Jones, in 2004. Built in 1936 and located on Sloane Square, this world-renowned store is a distinctive Grade II listed Modernist building. The building was sensitively altered with dramatic new interiors and extensions. As well as improved building services and operational facilities, John McAslan + Partners preserved the building's much loved and distinctive form. The project, completed in three phases, allowed operational continuity throughout the works and drew strong praise from the client and key authorities.

PROJECT FACTS

Address: Sloane Square, London SW1, United Kingdom. **Structural engineers:** Hurst Peirce Malcolm.
Client: John Lewis Partnership. **Completion:** 2004. **Gross floor area:** 30,000 m².

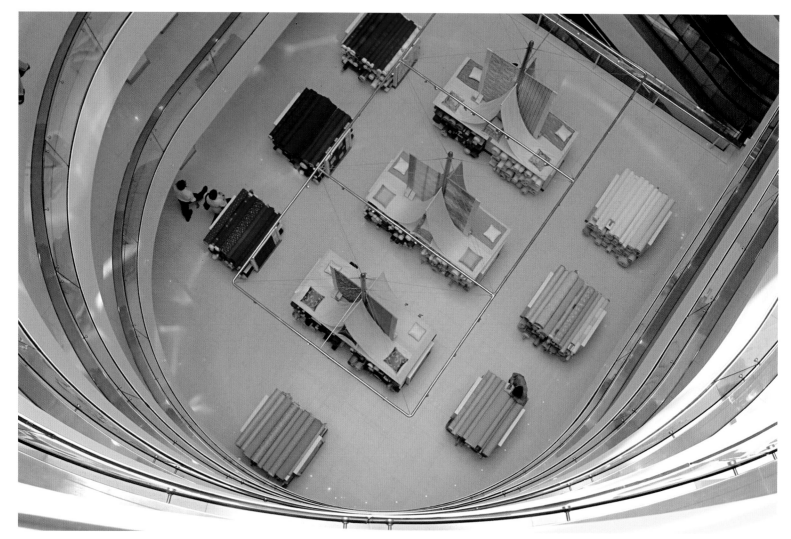

↑ | **Displays,** from above
← | **Large atrium,** permits views into other levels

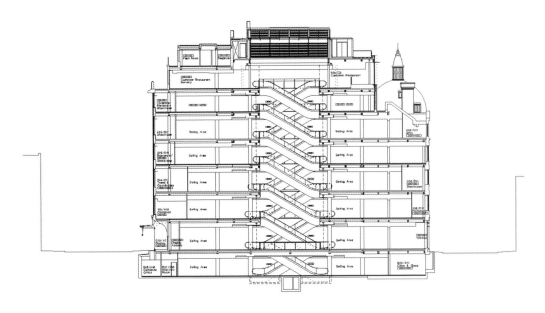

↖ | Section
↙ | Skylight, from below
↓ | White, modern interior, gives the center a
bright and welcoming character

schmidt hammer lassen
architects

↑ | **Entrance area**
↗ | **Interior view,** play of light
→ | **Green façades**

Caroli Shopping Center

Malmö

This project is based on recreating the qualities sof the original neighborhood before the center was built; with a focus on small squares, narrow streets, corridors and surprising urban spaces to evoke the feeling of a more intimate urban space. Small shifts and displacements in the façade break down the scale at eye level, creating small niches for impulsive gatherings. The addition of hallways, new entrances and exits enhance the feeling of openness and draw passers-by inside. Architecturally, the new Caroli will feature bright, inviting spaces with simple, functional and sustainable solutions. Pronounced use of daylight creates a bright, pleasant indoor climate while reducing energy consumption.

PROJECT FACTS

Address: Östergatan 12, 20011 Malmö, Sweden. **Original building:** Torsten Roos Arkitektkontor, 1973.
Client: Carnegie Fastigheter Sverige AB. **Completion:** 2013. **Gross floor area:** 25,000 m².

↑ | **Shopping passage**
← | **Ground floor plan**

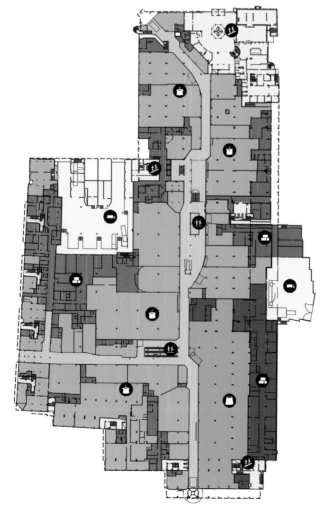

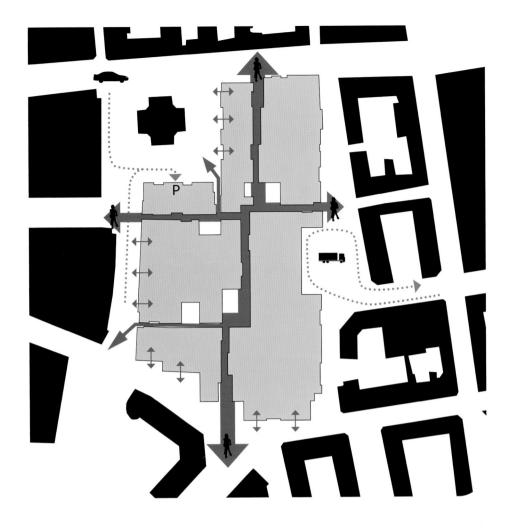

↖ | Site plan
↓ | Interior hall

Studio Daniel Libeskind

↑ | **Bird's-eye view**
↗ | **Street view**, at night
→ | **Interior**

Crystals in the Citycenter

Las Vegas

The crystalline and metal clad façade of Crystals signals to visitors well in advance of arrival that it is not a traditional retail environment. From the interior, the roof's dramatic angles and skylights become a backdrop for the luxury retail and dining it houses which include Louis Vuitton, Tiffany & Co., and Bulgari as well as concept restaurants from Wolfgang Puck and Todd English. The design and construction of Crystals employed the most environmentally conscious practices and materials. In November 2009 it was announced that Crystals achieved LEED Gold Core and Shell certification from the U.S. Green Building Council (USGBC), making it the world's largest retail district to receive this level of recognition.

PROJECT FACTS

Address: 3720 South Las Vegas Boulevard, Las Vegas, NV 89158, USA. **Structural engineers:** Halcrow Yolles. **Interior designers:** Rockwell Group. **Façade designers:** Israel Berger & Associates. **Collaborating architects:** Foster and Partners, Gensler, Murphy Jahn Architects, KPF, Pelli Clarke Pelli Architects, HKS, Leo A. Daly, RV Architecture, Adamson Associates Architects. **Client:** MGM Mirage. **Completion:** 2009. **Gross floor area:** 46,452 m². **Additional functions:** casino, hotels, residential.

↑ | Bird's-eye view
← | Interior

← | **Exterior night view,** with projecting lights
↓ | **Sketch**

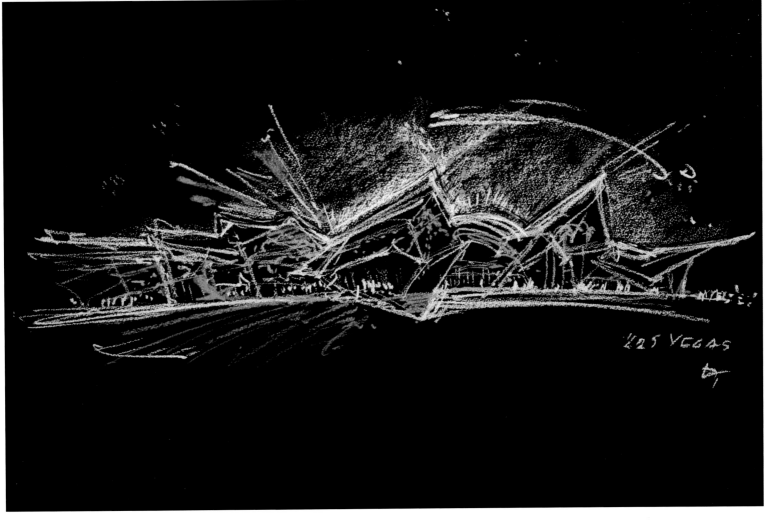

Aranguren & Gallegos
Arquitectos

↑ | **Interior view**

Ataranzas Municipal Market Restoration

Málaga

This project involved the rehabilitation and recovery of Ataranzas Central Market, as well as an substituting existing stalls, unable to meet today's requirements. The project aimed to recover the original design of the old Market, enhancing its character and architectural monumentality. In order to recover the original building scheme, all later additions have been demolished, re-establishing the visual connection of the axis between the door and large window. The design of the stalls references a large industrial structure from Donald Judd that comprises a sequence of tables upon which a sculptural series of basic color boxes are deposited. These have been constructed with metal paneled inside with corrugated iron on the outside with a series of basic color boxes.

Address: Calle De Las Ataranzas 10, Málaga, Spain. **Original building:** Rucoba, late 19th century.
Completion: 2010. **Gross floor area:** 3,194 m².

↑ | **Façade detail**
↓ | **Market stalls,** color boxes

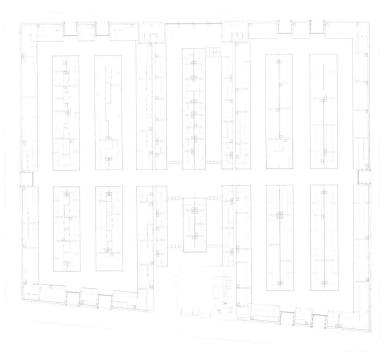

↑ | **Ground floor plan**

↑ | **Floating ensemble,** in the evening
↓ | **Arrangement**

mARkeT

River Maas

This project, designed by Andrea Sollazzo, Lucía Giménez and Anna Sarnowska, of Long Lie Architects, involved the creation of an art market is not only the creation of a shopping area: it is a place where artists and public come together, where they meet, talk, exchange ideas. At the same time, it is a place where the artists can find inspiration, a livable working environment, where they can easily find solitude. It is the creation of a microcosm, of a small society, a representation of two worlds colliding. From an architectural point of view, the challenge was creating a comfortable floating sustainable space that can aggregate and disaggregate, according to the actual conditions. There are two kind of modules that can be opened: one for the smaller shops/atelier, for the café, the administration and the service spaces that create the core of the market in a kind of village/labyrinth configuration, while the other module opens as a kind of tentacle to reach the land.

PROJECT FACTS
Address: along the River Maas. **Client:** Opgap. **Completion:** competition. **Gross floor area:** 80 m².

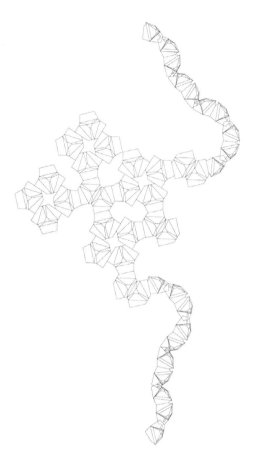

↑ | **Layout plan**
↓ | **Solar panels on market module**

↑ | **View,** from above

↑ | **Shopping mall**
↗ | **Pedestrian area**
→ | **Main view**

La Caserne de Bonne

Grenoble

The Bonne barracks were a former military site handed over to the city for the creation of an urban development zone. The development program for the former barracks, located between the city center and the Grands Boulevards, offers new social housing units, a school, green spaces, a cinema and a shopping mall. With this project, the architects aimed to increase the appeal of Grenoble's city center and contribute to its extension while supporting sustainable, responsible urban development. Considerable efforts have been made to ensure that the building integrates high performance sustainable development solutions by, for example, ensuring that the southern elevations remain largely transparent. An inward-looking and impenetrable military site will be turned into a new and welcoming neighborhood open to the city.

PROJECT FACTS

Address: 48, boulevard Gambetta, 38000 Grenoble, France. **Landscape architects:** Jaqueline Osty. **Urban planning commercial zone:** Christian Devillers, Aktis. **Client:** SCI Caserne de Bonne, Casino, Mercialys Group. **Completion:** 2010. **Gross floor area:** 25,500 m². **Additional functions:** offices, student residences.

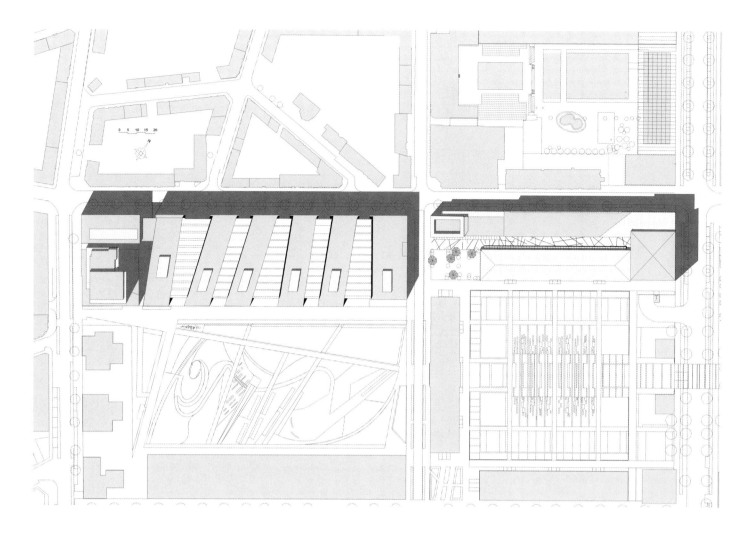

↑ | **Site plan**
← | **Rear view of the mall,** with a large public garden

← | **Shopping mall,** open-air
↓ | **Main view,** by night

↑ | **Bird's-eye view**
→ | **Entrance**

Starhill Gallery

Kuala Lumpur

Starhill Gallery is perhaps Kuala Lumpur's most iconic shopping mall, featuring an extraordinary array of luxury shops and fine dining restaurants. Spark's design proposal dealt with the reinvention of the existing façade by creating a visually interesting shop front, which embraces cutting edge technology and wraps the existing building in a crystalline skin of glass and stone panels. The fractured variation of solidity and transparency transforms the street façade of the existing building entirely, giving it a new contemporary classic identity that stands out amongst the 'quick-fix', ubiquitous shopping mall façades of many of Starhill Gallery's neighbors.

Address: 181, Jalan Bukit Bintang, 55100, Kuala Lumpur, Malaysia. **Client:** YTL Corporation Sdn Bhd 4. **Completion:** 2011. **Gross floor area of retail extension:** 2,000 m².

↑ | **Illuminated façade**
← | **Crystalline façade** of glass and stone panels

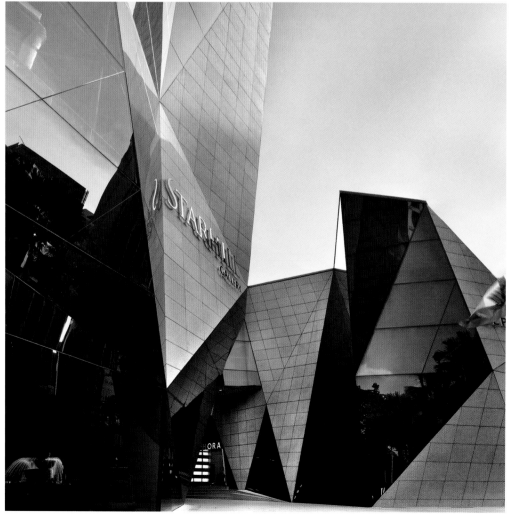

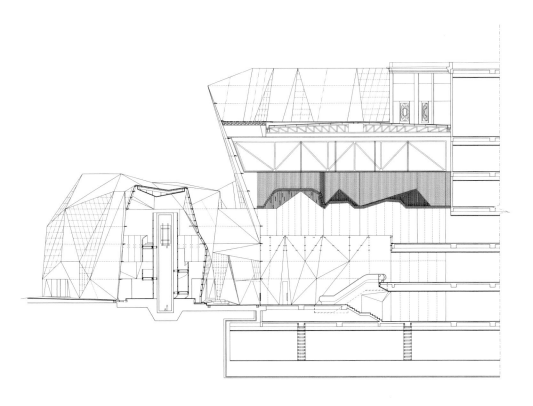

↖ | Section
↓ | Ground floor plan

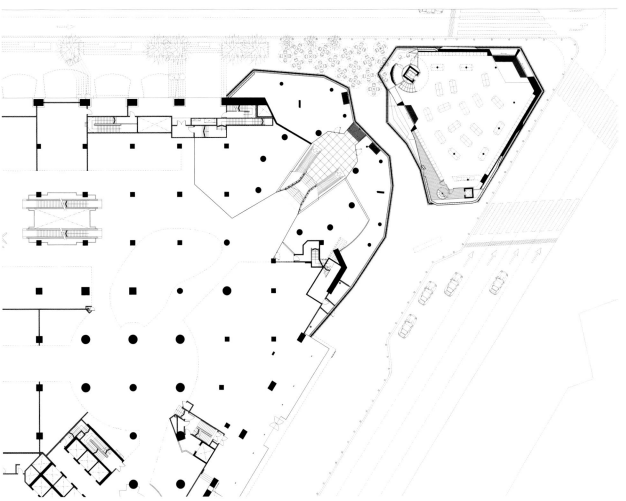

oliv architekten und
ingenieure

↑ | **Käfer delicatessen market**
→ | **Interior view,** market stalls

Schrannenhalle Market at the Viktualienmarkt

Munich

The renovation of the Schrannenhalle market hall is a big part of the design concept for the entire ensemble. The market hall is envisaged as an important addition to the Viktualienmarkt. It has its own independent architectural style that brings high quality products and market traditions to the fore. The Käfer market restaurant, a delicatessen with tasting and productions such as market stalls, restaurants and independent retailers are all united under one roof. A new market space has been developed that can be flexibly combined and assembled in different ways. The core area is surrounded by individual modules that allow a variety of uses from presentation of goods to refrigerated displays.

PROJECT FACTS **Address:** Viktualienmarkt 15, 80331 Munich, Germany. **Original building:** Karl Muffat, 1853. **Client:** Hammer AG, Michael Käfer. **Completion:** 2011. **Gross floor area:** 2,600 m². **Estimated visitors:** 5,000 per day.

↑ | **Café**
← | **Entrance**

← | Käfer market restaurant
↓ | Ground floor plan
↓↓ | Section

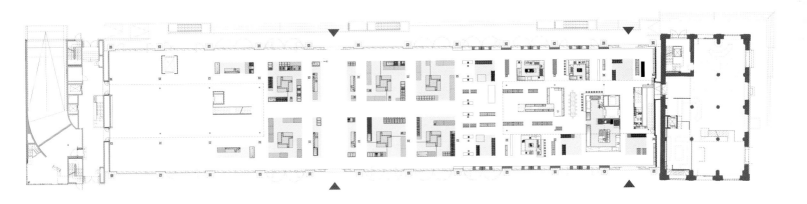

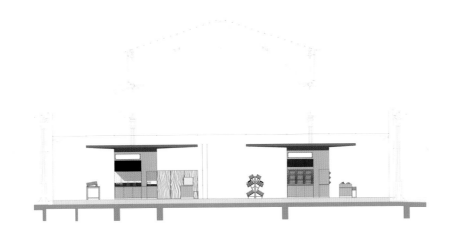

Index

Archi

tects' Index

10 Design
Gordon Affleck

3/F East Town Building, 41 Lockhart Road, Wanchai
Hong Kong (China)
T +852.39752010
F +852.39752000
press@10design.co
www.10design.co

3deluxe in/exterior
Andreas Lauhoff, Dieter Brell, Peter Seipp, Stephan
Lauhoff

Schwalbacherstraße 74
65183 Wiesbaden (Germany)
T +49.611.9522050
F +49.611.95220522
inexterior@3deluxe.de
www.3deluxe.de

A4 Studio
Géza Kendik, Viktória Dóczy, Péter Veszelik

Hegyi utca 1
1026 Budapest (Hungary)
T +36.139.27887
F +36.139.27888
studioa4@t-online.hu
www.a4studio.hu

Afarai
Afaina de Jong

Oudekerksplein 30
1012 GZ Amsterdam (The Netherlands)
info@afarai.com
www.afarai.com

Aflalo e Gasperini Arquitetos

Rua Helena 235
04552-050 São Paulo (Brazil)
T +55.5511.30407200
F +55.5511.30407213
ag@aflaloegasperini.com.br
www.aflaloegasperini.com.br

Ron Arad Architects

62 Chalk Farm Road
London NW1 8AN (United Kingdom)
T +44.207.2844963
info@ronarad.com
www.ronarad.co.uk

Aranguren & Gallegos Arquitectos SL
José González Gallegos, María José Aranguren Lopez

Calle Otero y Delage 118
28035 Madrid (Spain)
T +34.91.7341901
F +34.91.3160811
arquitectos@arangurengallegos.com
www.arangurengallegos.com

Architectural practice Arhis
Andris Kronbergs, Dace Gräve, Vilnis Uzors, Brigita Bula,
Baiba Liepiņa

Skarnu street 4
1050 Riga (Latvia)
T +371.67225852
F +371.67814141
arhis@arhis.lv
www.arhis.lv

Arup

13 Fitzroy Street
London W1T 4BQ (United Kingdom)
T +44.20.76361531
london@arup.com
www.arup.com

atelier ww
Kurt Hangarter, Danilo Morellini, Walter Wäschle, Rolf
Wüst, Urs Wüst

Asylstrasse 108
8032 Zurich (Switzerland)
T +41.44.3886666
F +41.44.3886616
buero@atelier-ww.ch
www.atelier-ww.ch

ATP Architects and Engineers

Heiliggeiststraße 16
6010 Innsbruck (Austria)
T +43.512.53700
F +43.512.53702194
info_ibk@atp.ag
www.www.atp.ag

B+W architecture sa, Ueli Brauen + Doris Wälchli
Doris Wälchli, Ueli Brauen

8, place de l'Europe
1003 Lausanne (Switzerland)
T +41.21.3406000
F +41.21.3406010
mail@bw-arch.ch
www.bw-arch.ch

BDP

PO Box 85, 11 Ducie Street
Manchester M60 3JA (United Kingdom)
enquiries@bdp.com
www.bdp.com

Benthem Crouwel Architekten
Joost Vos, Mels Crouwel, Jan Benthem, Marcel Blom,
Marten Wassmann, Markus Sporer

Bendstraße 50–52
52066 Aachen (Germany)
T +49.241.559450
F +49.241.5594520
bca@benthemcrouwel.de
www.benthemcrouwel.de

Blaser Architekten AG
Vinzenz Reist, Emanuela Britt, Christian W. Blaser

Austrasse 24
4051 Basel (Switzerland)
T +41.61.2789555
F +41.61.2789550
mail@blaserarchitekten.ch
www.blaserarchitekten.ch

Blocher Blocher Partners
Dieter Blocher, Jutta Blocher

Herdweg 19
70174 Stuttgart (Germany)
T +49.711.22 4820
F +49.711.22 48220
info@blocherblocher.com
www.blocherblocher.com

Blocher Blocher India Pvt. Ltd.
Dieter Blocher, Jutta Blocher

C-37, Connaught Place
New Delhi 110001 (India)
T +91.99.71878849
india@blocherblocher.com
www.blocherblocher.com

Buro II & Archi+I

Bellevue 5, 7th floor
9050 Gent-Ledeberg (Belgium)
T +32.09.2101710
info@b2ai.com
www.b2ai.com

Chapman Taylor

Paseo de Recoletos 16, 7th floor
28001 Madrid (Spain)
T +34.91.4170925
F +34.91.417.0926

Design International
Davide Padoa

20–22 Stukeley Street
London WC2B 5LR (United Kingdom)
T +44.20.70922700
F +44.20.70922799
london@designinternational.com
www.designinternational.com

Despang Architekten
Günther Despang, Martin Despang, Cynthia Despang,
Isabel Schlüpmann

Hölderlinstraße 9
01445 Radebeul (Germany)
info@despangarchitekten.de
www.despangarchitekten.de

Diener & Diener Architekten
Roger Diener

Henric Petri-Strasse 22
4010 Basel (Switzerland)
T +41.61.2704141
F +41.61.2704100
buero.basel@dienerdiener.ch
www.dienerdiener.ch

Architekten Domenig & Wallner

Jahngasse 9/I
8010 Graz (Austria)
T +43.316.827753
F +43.316.827753-9
office@domenig-wallner.at
www.domenig-wallner.at

DP Architects

6 Raffles Boulevard, 04-100 Marina Square
039594 Singapore (Singapore)
T +65.6338.3988
F +65.6337.9989
dparchitects@dpa.com.sg
www.dpa.com.sg

ECE Projektmanagement G.m.b.H & Co. KG

Heegbarg 30
22391 Hamburg (Germany)
T +49.40.606060
F +49.40.606066230
info@ece.com
www.ece.com

Iñaki Echeverria

Homero 820
11560 Polanco (Mexico)
T +52.55.55311303
studio@inakiecheverria.com
www.inakiecheverria.com

Erick van Egeraat

Calandstraat 23
3016 CA Rotterdam (The Netherlands)
info@erickvanegeraat.com
www.erickvanegeraat.com

Elliott + Associates Architects
Rand Elliott, David Ketch

35 Harrison Avenue
Oklahoma City, OK 73104 (USA)
T +1.405.2329554
F +1.405.2329997
design@e-a-a.com
www.e-a-a.com

ERA

Gardenya Plaza 3 Kat:8 Atasehir
34758 Istanbul (Turkey)
T +90.216.4559209
era@era-arch.com
www.era-arch.com

form A architekten

Vondelstraße 29–31
50677 Cologne (Germany)
T +49.221.25080790
F +49.221.25080799
www.form-a.de

Foster + Partners
Norman Foster

22 Hester Road
London SW11 4AN (United Kingdom)
T +44.20.77380455
F +44.20.77381107
info@fosterandpartners.com
www.fosterandpartners.com

GAD - Global Architectural Developement

Gokhan Avcioglu

Tesvikiye Cad. 3B Gunes Apt.
34367 Istanbul (Turkey)
T +90.212.3275125
F +90.212.2581663
gad@gadarchitecture.com
www.gadarchitecture.com

Manuelle Gautrand Architecture

36, boulevard de la Bastille
75012 Paris (France)
T +33.1.56950646
F +33.1.56950647
contact-com@manuelle-gautrand.com
www.manuelle-gautrand.com

José Fernando Gonçalves

Rua Eugénio de Castro 248
4100-225 Porto (Portugal)
T +351.22.6060179
jfgarquitectos@sapo.pt
www.josefernandogoncalves.com

Architekturbüro Ute Göschel

Westerhamer Straße 2
83620 Feldkirchen-Westerham (Germany)
T +49.8063.973600
F +49.8063.9736012
info@architekturbuero-utegoeschel.de
www.architekturbuero-utegoeschel.de

→ 64

Granz & Zecher Architekten
Joachim Zecher, Christoph Beck, Frank Bielka, Horst
Buschkowsky, Bernd Niewienda

Dircksenstraße 46
10178 Berlin (Germany)
T +49.30.28044660
F +49.30.280446610
info@gz-architekten.de
www.gz-architekten.de

→ 168

groupe-6
Mark Wilson

94, avenue Ledru-Rollin
75011 Paris (France)
T +33.1.53179600
F +33.1.53179636
paris@groupe-6.com
www.groupe-6.com

→ 220, 276, 290, 400

Zaha Hadid Architects

10 Bowling Green Lane
London EC1R 0BQ (United Kingdom)
T +44.20.72535147
F +44.20.72518322
press2@zaha-hadid.com
www.zaha-hadid.com

→ 34, 100

Haskoll (Beijing) Architectural Design Consultancy
Peter Goldsmith

Unit 1516, 15/F Office Tower Beijing Guangming Hotel
42 Liangmaqiao Road, Chaoyang District
Beijing 100125 (China)
T +86.10.65330622
F +86.10.65330523
pr@haskoll.cn
www.haskoll.cn

→ 244

Helin & Co Architects
Hanna Euro, Harri Koski, Pekka Helin

Urho Kekkosen katu 3 B
00101 Helsinki (Finland)
T +358.20.7577800
F +358.20.7577801
info@helinco.fi
www.helinco.fi

→ 30

HOK
Barry Hughes, Vance Thompson

Qube, 90 Whifield Street
London W1T 4EZ (United Kingdom)
T +44.20.76362006
F +44.20.76361987
HOKContact@hok.com
www.hok.com

→ 326

HPP Hentrich–Petschnigg & Partner GmbH + Co. KG
Joachim H. Faust, Gerhard G. Feldmeyer, Remigiusz
Otrzonsek, Werner Sübai, Gerd Heise, Volker Weuthen

Kaistraße 5
40221 Dusseldorf (Germany)
T +49.211.83840
F +49.211.8384185
duesseldorf@hpp.com
www.hpp.com

→ 218

HPP International Planungsgesellschaft mbH
Joachim H. Faust, Gerhard G. Feldmeyer, Remigiusz
Otrzonsek, Werner Sübai, Gerd Heise, Volker Weuthen

Kaistraße 5
40221 Düsseldorf (Germany)
+49.211.83840
+49.211.8384185
international@hpp.com
www.hpp.com

→ 14

Huss Hawlik Architekten
Ernst Huss, Andreas Hawlik

Neuwaldeggerstraße 14
1170 Vienna (Austria)
T +43.1.489 6260
F +43.1.489 6273
office@huss-hawlik.at
www.huss-hawlik.at

→ 96

Ibelings van Tilburg Architecten
Aat van Tilburg, Martin Schoenmakers, Marc Ibelings

Veerhaven 7
3016 CJ Rotterdam (The Netherlands)
T +31.10.2021900
F +31.10.2021999
info@ibelingsvantilburg.nl
www.ibelingsvantilburg.nl

→ 364

Jacobs-Yaniv Architects
Tamar Jacobs, Oshri Yaniv

65 Sokolov Street
47218 Ramat Ha'sharon (Israel)
T +972.9.9541241
F +972.9.9571714
info@jacobs-yaniv.com
www.jacobs-yaniv.com

→ 280

The Jerde Partnership
Sergio Zeballos, David Rogers, Eduardo Lopez

913 Ocean Front Walk
Venice, CA 90291 (USA)
T +1.310.3991987
F +1.310.3921316
busdev@jerde.com
www.jerde.com

→ 180, 348, 360

Jourdan & Müller · PAS
Jochem Jourdan, Bernhard Müller,
Benjamin Jourdan

Brönnerstraße 9
60313 Frankfurt/Main (Germany)
T +49.69.9708180
F +49.69.97081811
mail@jourdan-mueller.de
www.jourdan-mueller.de

→ 338

Dara Kirmizitoprak Architecture

Eski Büyükdere Cad. Ayazağa Yolu Giz Plaza
34367 Istanbul (Turkey)
T +90.212.2906660
info@darakirmizitoprak.com

→ 56

Klein Dytham architecture (KDa)
Astrid Klein, Mark Dytham

AD Bldg. 2F, 1-15-7 Hiroo
150-0012 Shibuya-ku, Tokyo (Japan)
T +81.357.952277
F +81.357.952276
kda@klein-dytham.com
www.klein-dytham.com

→ 372

L35 Architects
Caterina Memeo, Nina Muzio, Eduardo Simarro, Patricia
Zymanis, Pamela Martín, Sonia Sanz, Jos Galán

Avinguda Diagonal 466 6ª planta
08006 Barcelona (Spain)
T +34.93.2922299
F +34.93.4160530
L35@L35.com
www.L35.com

→ 202, 260, 318

Studio Daniel Libeskind

2 Rector street 19th floor
New York, NY 10006 (USA)
T +1.212.4979100
F +1.212.2852130
info@daniel-libeskind.com
www.daniel-libeskind.com

→ 18, 380, 392

Lifschutz Davidson Sandilands
Alex Lifschutz, Paul Sandilands

Island Studios, 22 St Peter's Square
London W6 9NW (United Kingdom)
T +44.208.6004800
F +44.208.6004700
mail@lds-uk.com
www.lds-uk.com

→ 352

Liong Lie Architects

Sint-Jobsweg 30
3024 EJ Rotterdam (The Netherlands)
T +31.10.4782064
info@lionglie.com
www.lionglie.com

→ 398

peterlorenzateliers

Maria-Theresien-Straße 37
6020 Innsbruck (Austria)
T +43.1.5334908
F +43.1.533490817
office@peterlorenz.at
www.peterlorenz.at

→ 88, 248

John McAslan + Partners

7–9 William Road
London NW1 3ER (United Kingdom)
T +44.20.7313600
F +44.20.7313601
marketing@mcaslan.co.uk
www.mcaslan.co.uk

Josep Mias Architects

Calle Mateu 19 bxs
08012 Barcelona (Spain)
T +34.93.2388208
F +34.93.2388209
miasmail@miasarquitectes.com
www.miasarchitects.com

Migdal Arquitectos/Jaime Varon, Abraham Metta, Alex Metta

Avenida Prolongacion Paseo de la Reforma 1236, piso 11, Colonia Santa Fe, Deleg Cuajimalpa
05348 Mexico City (Mexico)
T +52.155.91770177
F +52.155.91770170
gcaballero@migdal.com.mx
www.migdal.com.mx

C.F. Møller Architects

Mads Mandrup, Klaus Toustrup, Mads Møller, Michael Kruse, Lone Wiggers, Julian Weyer, Klavs Hyttel, Anna Maria Indrio, Tom Danielsen

Europaplads 2, 11
8000 Aarhus C (Denmark)
T +45.7305300
cfmoller@cfmoller.com
www.cfmoller.com

MVRDV

Winy Maas, Jacob van Rijs, Nathalie de Vries

PO Box 63136
3002 JC Rotterdam (The Netherlands)
T +31.10.4772860
F +31.10.4773627
office@mvrdv.nl
www.mvrdv.nl

NIO architecten

Maurice Nio, Joan Almekinders

Schiedamse Vest 95a
3012 BG Rotterdam (The Netherlands)
T +31.10.4122318
F +31.10.4126075
nio@nio.nl
www.nio.nl

O&O Baukunst

Harry Lutz, Laurids Ortner, Florian Matzker, Manfred Ortner, Christian Heuchel, Markus Penell, Roland Duda

Am Modenapark 6/11
1030 Vienna (Austria)
T +43.1.5232812
F +43.1.523281228
baukunst@ortner-ortner.com
www.ortner-ortner.com

ofis

Špela Videčnik, Rok Oman

Tavcarjeva 2
1000 Ljubljana (Slovenia)
T +386.1.4260084
F +386.1.4260085
ofis@ofis.si
www.ofis-a.si

oliv architekten und ingenieure

Thomas Sutir

Sonnenstraße 6
80331 Munich (Germany)
T +49.89.53 90 63 870
F +49.89.53 90 63 879
info@oliv-architekten.de
www.oliv-architekten.com

ONL

Essenburgsingel 94c
3022 EG Rotterdam (The Netherlands)
T +31.10.2447039
F +31.10.2447041
onl@oosterhuis.nl
www.oosterhuis.nl

Pascal Arquitectos

Carlos Pascal, Gerard Pascal

Atlaltunco 99, Colonia Lomas de Tecamachalco
53970 Mexico City CP (Mexico)
T +52.55.52942371
F +52.55.52948513
carlos@pascalarquitectos.com
www.pascalarquitectos.com

Peña architecture
Gabriel Raúl Peña

Wijnbrugstraat 184
3011 XW Rotterdam (The Netherlands)
F +31.10.4258083
info@pena-architecture.com
www.pena-architecture.com

pos4 Hinrichsmeyer Pilling GbR
Ulrich Hinrichsmeyer, André Pilling

Prinz-Georg-Straße 126
40479 Düsseldorf (Germany)
T +49.211.1623472
F +49.211.1623474
info@pos4.de
www.www.pos4.de

Promontorio
João Luís Ferreira, Pedro Appleton, Paulo Perloiro, João Perloiro, Paulo Martins Barata

Rua Fabrica Material de Guerra 10
1950-128 Lisbon (Portugal)
T +351.218.620970
F +351.218.620971
ana@promontorio.net
www.www.promontorio.net

Radionica Arhitekture
Ana Boljar, Marusja Tus, Vedrana Ivanda, Nenad Ravnic, Goran Rako, Josip Sabolic, Kata Marunica, Kristina Jeren

Crnomerec 135
10000 Zagreb (Croatia)
T +385.1.3778567
F +385.1.3778568
info@radionica-arhitekture.hr
www.radionica-arhitekture.hr

Ramseier & Associates Ltd.
Andreas Ramseier

Utoquai 43
8008 Zurich (Switzerland)
T +41.44.2509999
ramseier@ramseier-assoc.com
www.ramseier-assoc.com

Ravetllat - Ribas
Carme Ribas, Pere Joan Ravetllat

Rambla Catalunya 11, Principal 2ª
08007 Barcelona (Spain)
rqr@coac.net
www.ravetllatribas.com

Rios Clementi Hale Studios
Julie Smith-Clementi, Mark Rios, Frank Clementi, Bob Hale

639 North Larchmont Boulevard, Suite 100
Los Angeles, CA 90004 (USA)
T +1.323.7851800
F +1.323.7851842
amanda@rchstudios.com
www.rchstudios.com

RKW Rhode Kellermann Wawrowsky Architektur + Städtebau
Dieter Schmoll

Tersteegenstraße 30
40474 Dusseldorf (Germany)
T +49.211.43670
F +49.211.4367111
info@rkwmail.de
www.rkw-as.de

rojkind arquitectos
Michel Rojkind, Gerardo Salinas

Tamaulipas 30 Piso 12, Colonia Hipodromo Condesa
06170 Mexico City CP (Mexico)
T +52.55.52808396
F +52.55.52808521
info@rojkindarquitectos.com
www.rojkindarquitectos.com

RTKL Associates

2101 L Street North-West, Suite 200
Washington, DC 20037 (USA)
T +1.202.8334400
F +1.202.8875168
dvican@rtkl.com
www.rtkl.com

Schiller Architektur BDA
Patrick Schiller

Bünzwanger Strasse 6/2
73066 Uhingen (Germany)
T +49.7161.31018
F +49.7161.33928
info@schiller-architektur.de
www.schiller-architektur.de

schmidt hammer lassen architects
Kristian Lars Ahlmark

Aaboulevarden 37
8000 Aarhus C (Denmark)
T +45.86201900
F +45.86184513
info@shl.dk
www.shl.dk

Spark
Stephen Pimbley

8 Murray Street 01–02, Murray Terrace
Singapore 079522 (Singapore)
info@sparkarchitects.com
www.sparkarchitects.com

T+T Design

Hanzeweg 16
2803 MC Gouda (The Netherlands)
T +31.182.690900
F +31.182.690690
office-nl@multi-development.com

UNStudio
Ben van Berkel

Stadhouderskade 113
1073 AX Amsterdam (The Netherlands)
T +31.20.5702040
F +31.20.5702041
info@unstudio.com
www.unstudio.com

Vitruvius & Sons
Sergey Padalko, Dmitry Melentyev, Oleg Kosenko, Alexey Solovyev

Bolshaya Morskaya Street 49 A
1-H St. Petersburg (Russia)
T +7.812.3145009
F +7.812.3126378
vitruviosons@yandex.ru
www.vitruviosons.com

Wingårdh Arkitektkontor AB
Gert Wingårdh, Cecilia Strömn

Kungsgatan 10A
41119 Göteborg (Sweden)
T +46.31.7437000
F +46.31.7119838
wingardhs@wingardhs.se
www.wingardhs.se

Winking · Froh Architekten BDA
Martin Froh, Bernhard Winking

Sophienstraße 22a
10178 Berlin (Germany)
T +49.30.2830280
F +49.30.28302828
berlin@winking-froh.de
www.winking-froh.de

WOHA
Richard Hassell, Wong Mun Summ

29 Hong Kong Street
Singapore 059668 (Singapore)
T +65.6423.4555
F +65.6423.4666
admin@woha.net
www.woha.net

Zechner & Zechner ZT GmbH
Christoph Zechner, Martin Zechner

Stumpergasse 14/23
1060 Wien (Austria)
T +43.1.59703360
F +43.1.597033699
email@zechner.com
www.zechner.com

All other pictures were made available by the architects.

Cover front: Patrick Bingham-Hall
Cover back: left: Lin Ho
right: Patrik Gunnar Helin, Allingsås

IMPRINT

The Deutsche Nationalbibliothek lists this publication in
the Deutsche Nationalbibliografie; detailed bibliographic
data are available in the Internet at http://dnb.dnb.de

ISBN 978-3-03768-154-1

© 2014 by Braun Publishing AG
www.braun-publishing.ch

1st edition 2014

Selection of projects: Editorial office van Uffelen
Layout and text editing: Judith Felten, Lisa Rogers, Lisa
Schaber, Clara Vogel
Graphic concept: ON Grafik | Tom Wibberenz
Reproduction: Bild1Druck GmbH, Berlin